TEAMING UP

ACHIEVING ORGANIZATIONAL
TRANSFORMATION

D0311496

TEAMING UP

ACHIEVING ORGANIZATIONAL TRANSFORMATION

Carl L. Harshman and
Steven L. Phillips

Amsterdam • Johannesburg • London
San Diego • Sydney • Toronto

© Copyright 1994 by Carl L. Harshman and Steven L. Phillips

Pfeiffer & Company
8517 Production Avenue
San Diego, CA 92121-2280 USA

Copyright under International, Pan American, and Universal Copyright Conventions. All rights reserved. No part of this book may be reproduced or transmitted in any form or by any means, electronic or mechanical, including photocopying, recording, or any information storage-and-retrieval system, without written permission from the publisher. Brief passages (not to exceed 1,000 words) may be quoted for reviews.

This publication is designed to provide accurate and authoritative information in regard to the subject matter covered. It is sold with the understanding that the publisher is not engaged in rendering legal, accounting, or other professional service. If legal advice or other expert assistance is required, the services of a competent professional person should be sought. *From a Declaration of Principles jointly adopted by a Committee of the American Bar Association and a Committee of Publishers.*

Page Compositor: Galen Bancroft/Russell Enterprises
Cover: Tom Lewis, Inc.

ISBN: Trade Paper 0-89384-237-0
        Hardcover 0-88390-411-X

Printed in the United States of America.

1 2 3 4 5 6 7 8 9 10

CONTENTS

ACKNOWLEDGMENTS

This book is a product of years of reading, thinking, and most importantly experience. It would not have been possible to generate the product without all three.

Several people in higher education impacted early thinking about knowledge, organizations, and people. One was Harold B. Pepinsky, the noted psychologist. Pep was the major force in breaking down old barriers of knowledge in the form of disciplines and opening up new horizons to learning. The other was C. DeWitt Hardy, professor and humanitarian. DeWitt's perspectives on people (positive) and organizations (less than positive) created an awakening about what organizations could and should be like. Edward E. Lawler III, Tom Cummings, and the faculty of the Center for Effective Organizations at the University of Southern California provided much insight and direction to the concepts of change in large organizations.

Much of the initial work in, and model for, organizational change was influenced by W. Patrick Dolan, a mentor and an extraordinary consultant. Pat's ability to integrate liberal learning with the real world and to connect it to the American workplace provided a unique opportunity to try new things. Pat's inspiration and early work in bringing management and labor together opened new doors to joint processes that will never again be closed.

Peter Block, a friend and colleague, bolstered persistence amid frustration with the writing. Peter's views of people and organizations also provided a regular sounding board (even when we do not like some of the sounds) and his experiences as an author served as a benchmark that "we're not in this alone."

We are also deeply indebted to the efforts of our friend, Cindy Krepky, who provided early editorial assistance and pointed out the rocks and shoals in the fog of initial drafts. Dick Roe and JoAnn Padgett of Pfeiffer & Company were both encouraging and helpful along the way. Without them, the work would not have been possible.

Finally, we believe that the strength of the work lies in its position between theory and practice. Of course without the corporations and unions with which we have worked, and the thousands of wonderful people who tolerated our learning and mistakes, we could not have come this far. We hope the contribution of the work in some way repays our debt to all of you.

Carl L. Harshman, Ph.D.
Steven L. Phillips, Ph.D.

PREFACE

American business and industry faced an almost insurmountable challenge during the 1980s. Having survived the ups and downs in the early part of the century, organizations experienced unprecedented growth for decades following World War II. But as the global context changed and old structures, practices, and relationships became less effective, American business was caught between the success of prior decades and the forces of a new economic and social paradigm.

Two theories explain the resulting dilemma. First, open systems theory (Katz and Kahn, 1982) predicts that in times of imbalance, a system—physical or social—will attempt to reestablish equilibrium based on its prior state. The recurring cycle of imbalance-rebalance is a condition called dynamic homeostasis. During periods of growth and when conditions causing instability are neither too intense nor too prolonged, the organization will tend to establish balance with incremental adjustments in the existing models or paradigms.

The problem for private or public sector organizations in the nineties is that the conditions creating imbalances—be they foreign competition, cuts in defense spending, taxpayer revolts, or the changing values of society—are both severe and persistent. Often, incremental adjustments in old models or paradigms will not solve the imbalance problem.

The second theory addresses how organizations respond to imbalance and why, at some point, those responses are not effective. Thomas Kuhn's (1984) notion of *paradigm* suggests that people tend to "see" the world in terms of old frameworks and to respond to it within pre-scribed limits and with familiar skills. The problem is that in a period of decline (or what in Kuhn's terms may be a "paradigm shift"), people may be seeing a new world for the first time (through obsolete lenses) and responding to this world with tools and practices that are no longer relevant. In this case, responding to periods of imbalance with the paradigms that made an organization successful in the prior era may actually speed, rather than inhibit, its decline. The American response to crisis often treats the symptoms rather than the problem. Strategies aimed at symptoms and based on old paradigms either gloss over or compound the real problem rather than provide perma-nent, effective solutions.

Three strategies are common to organizations in a state of prolonged imbalance.

- The Savior Syndrome—wishing and even searching for a Jack Welch (of General Electric) or a Lee Iacocca (of Chrysler) to save the organization.

- The Miracle Cure—hoping for the miracle "drug" to cure organizational ills and, in the meantime, trying every available off-the-shelf program in hopes that it will help.

- The Superman Syndrome—saying, "I've got it!" "It's under control" and all of the other telltale indicators of not understanding the problem.

These strategies come into play when old models and practices are no longer suited to the current context. At this point the organization encounters challenges unlike any it has faced in the past. Dealing with these challenges requires a change approach that is both reasonable and realistic. Doing what one always did will only work if what one has is what one had before.

The difficulty for organizations suffering from performance problems based on a changing context is twofold.

1. The milieu of the organization—internal and external—is far different from any encountered in the past, yet conditions and variables look as though they are merely variations on the past.

2. Approaches to dealing with organizational problems are grounded primarily in the classical, mechanical systems paradigms and are based on what solved such problems in the past.

Because most organizations are led and managed by professionals who were trained in the machine/mechanical paradigm of the 1940s and 1950s, they bring to the organization a linear perspective and the rational, logical model on which traditional systems are based. Difficulties arise because organizations are *not* only physical, mechanical, or monetary systems. The classic machine model of management, for example, in which people are only one component of the larger system, tends to underplay the human element of systems and to oversimplify the problem. More important, managers have been led to believe that the rational, logical, and deductive tools used to direct and control physical systems are also appropriate to the management and control of human systems. This is simply not the case!

Although the human and technical dimensions of organizations are intimately linked, the strategies for changing the two are significantly different. While most technical systems changes are based on planned, sequential, linear models, the transformation of human systems is neither sequential nor linear. As a result, organizations need an approach to change that acknowledges the unique characteristics of human systems and that addresses those differences in the pursuit of change.

Unfortunately, much of what is available either is theoretical and difficult to translate into practice or is practice that addresses only one or two facets of a complete situation faced by the organization. The impractical, irrelevant, or insufficient are of little value to the organization at the end of an era. Organizations in the United States need an approach to change and development that is comprehensive, practical, and effective. This book describes a model and an approach proven over the last decade to meet all three criteria.

Organization of This Book

Team-Based Organizational Change has been written for people at all levels of an organization that needs to change and that finds old approaches insufficient. It is written for the practitioner who has neither time nor inclination to read volumes about organizational theory, change, or tactics. It is intended to be used both in understanding the context of change and in developing approaches to make the change happen.

The book is organized in a modular format. Each module focuses on a concept to be learned or a task to be completed. Illustrations, tables, and exercises are used liberally to assist the reader in understanding the concepts. A short summary appears at the beginning of each module so that the key ideas can be easily and quickly extracted. The modules are presented in general chronological order from start to finish of the change effort. Many of the modules provide the reader with an opportunity to transfer the ideas to his or her organization.

This book is about changing organizations through use of a team-based strategy. It is oriented toward established, traditional organizations that, for reasons of survival or adaptation, find themselves in need of changing their culture from a top-down hierarchy to one that is flattened and empowered for improved overall performance. But, it is not a simple recipe for success; in fact, quite the opposite is true.

Changing organizations is neither quick nor easy. Change requires extensive understanding and commitment by leadership, whether that leadership is corporate or plant, management, labor, or staff. This book helps everyone from the first-line supervisor to the corporate executive understand the change context and how to deal with it. The aim is to provide a tool for planning and implementing the change process in your organization.

The framework of the book is based on (a) understanding where the organization is at present, (b) defining where it wants to be (the future), and (c) instituting a strategy and process that provides a means to get there. The first chapter discusses the characteristics of traditional and high-performance organizations and provides background on organizational behavior as it relates to change. It also introduces the theory of change and the strategy model used in a change process. The model is based on a set of principles and practices that have evolved from our work with a variety of organizations over the last decade.

The second chapter addresses planning for the change process. It describes the planning structure and the diagnostic process used to collect data for the plan. This chapter helps define the basis for the future of your organization. It also discusses the forces that drive organizations toward change and the barriers that prevent organizations from moving to the envisioned future.

Chapter 3 provides a description of the change management structure. This structure is responsible for designing and managing the change process. Chapter 4 describes a strategy, consisting of four elements, for the change process. These elements include determining the level of participation (i.e., team strategy), developing the leadership or business teams, assessing and developing organizational communication and business information systems, and resolving organizational issues. Chapter 5 offers guidance on implementing the strategy.

Once the change strategy has been implemented, the process must be managed. Such change management is covered in Chapter 6. Many barriers can slow or derail change efforts. These barriers are described in Chapter 7, along with means for dealing with them to get the change process back on track. Based on the concept of "stages of learning" in organizations, Chapter 8 discusses two types of learning and the role they play in organizational behavior and the change process.

Finally, there are appendixes devoted to two special topics. Appendix A focuses on the differences in implementing change processes in public versus private sector organizations. Appendix B deals with issues related to implementing a change process in unionized workplaces. We also have provided a list of suggested reading on topics related to team-based organizations and change.

1

CONSIDERATIONS FOR A TEAM-BASED CHANGE PROCESS

Characteristics of Traditional Organizations

A traditional organization functions as a top-down, authoritarian, control-based hierarchy. It is typically characterized by tightly held power; separate, often competitive functional departments; inadequate communication; control systems with quantitative, short-term, crisis-oriented time frames; and out-moded "carrot-and-stick" motivation systems.

Traditional organizations function by putting people in charge at the top and giving them the authority and responsibility to control the human and technical systems below. The structure operates through layers of management, with each layer having less authority than the one above. The resulting *top-down, authoritarian hierarchy* places control at the top and response mechanisms at the bottom.

The traditional structure is also defined by "gridding" the middle into functional organizations. The grids (or departments) represent specialties (such as finance, production, maintenance, engineering, marketing, sales, and customer service, that perform specific tasks. These departments have relatively well-defined boundaries and are encouraged to maintain tight control over their "piece of the system," thus, in essence, discouraging cooperation between functions. Department managers tend to be highly competitive and to focus on their own domains, giving little thought to the success of the overall organization.

Poor communication is common in traditional organizations. Information from the top consists primarily of *command-and-control* content. The amount of formal information flowing downward decreases as one moves toward the bottom of the structure; the lower one is in the organization, the less one "needs to know" about what is happening and why. Information (except for positive data) does

3

not move up the system well because perspectives from below are not valued. And since much of the information from below would be critical or threatening, the layers and grids within the organization serve as filters to "protect" the upper echelons. This protectionist tendency also inhibits the movement of information across the grids and between work groups at lower levels.

The traditional structure is also characterized by a *short-term, crisis-oriented time frame*, monitored and judged on the basis of immediate results (numbers). Problem solving tends to be poor and to be reactive, defensive, and symptom-driven. It is controlled by upper management, so participation in problem solving is less likely to be found at the lower levels of the organization.

Reward and punishment (*motivation*) systems tend to be fairly narrowly defined, and consequences are misaligned. In other words, positive reinforcement is given for negative behavior (such as giving the poor performer less work and responsibility), and negative consequences follow positive performance (such as giving the peak performer more work). Fear of punishment (or loss of job) is a primary driver for behavior and affects decision making, information exchange, and cooperation across departmental boundaries. In a traditional system, money and benefits are powerful motivators but have little to do with employee satisfaction, loyalty, caring, or willingness to contribute extra effort.

In traditional organizations, the mission is neither clearly understood nor accepted by the majority of the employees. In addition, traditional organizations often lack a clear and consensus-based vision. Even if there is a vision, the organization often fails to make a connection between the vision and major organization decisions and actions. As a result, goals tend to be short term and quantitative and may or may not be the basis for the overall planning process.

Traditional organizations also tend to be unable to make significant paradigm shifts; that is, they are incapable of learning. Change is incremental and is likely to conform to and reinforce the status quo. Tradition, or "the way things have been done in the past," is important, risk taking is not encouraged, and error brings severe consequences. Figure 1-1 summarizes the characteristics of the traditional structure. All of these characteristics tend to keep things as they are rather than change them to what they ought to be.

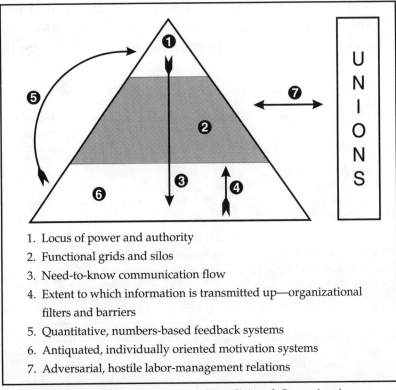

1. Locus of power and authority
2. Functional grids and silos
3. Need-to-know communication flow
4. Extent to which information is transmitted up—organizational filters and barriers
5. Quantitative, numbers-based feedback systems
6. Antiquated, individually oriented motivation systems
7. Adversarial, hostile labor-management relations

Figure 1-1. Characteristics of Traditional Organizations

Characteristics of
High-Performance Organizations

High-performance organizations differ from traditional
organizations in their guiding principles, structure,
work roles, operating procedures, communication
flow, and motivational methods.

The characteristics of high-performance organizations are
quite different from those of traditional organizations. Table 1-1 compares the two.

The high-performance organization philosophy is
oriented toward a vision of quality products and quality
work life. Inherent in this outlook is the notion that the
organization's human resources are its key asset in
achieving high levels of performance. Such a change in

Table 1-1. Traditional versus High-Performance Organizations

Guiding Principles in Traditional Organizations	Human Dimensions as Basis for Comparison	Guiding Principles in High-Performance Organizations
Authority is at the top of the organization. Decisions are passed down the chain of command.	Authority and Decision Making	Authority is well distributed. Decisions are made at the right level.
Focus is on *my* job or *our* department. Finger pointing, blaming prevail, with little integrated problem solving.	Focus and Cooperation	Focus is on success of the organization. Cooperation and problem solving are everywhere.
Control of information is at the top and in functional areas. Little business information is available at the lowest level. Available information often lacks credibility.	Information and Communication	Information flows up, down, and across. Appropriate business data are available at all levels. Information and sources are highly credible.

Table 1-1. Traditional versus High-Performance Organizations (continued)

Guiding Principles in Traditional Organizations	Human Dimensions as Basis for Comparison	Guiding Principles in High-Performance Organizations
Little or no data from the lowest level reach the upper levels. The structure is unresponsive.	Listening	Genuine listening occurs at all levels. The organization cares about and is responsive to the needs and requirements of business units and people.
Commitment to the success of the organization is "spotty" at best. Emphasis is on "external" rewards and motivators. Punishment and incentive system are dominant motivation tools.	Commitment and Motivation	Commitment to goals and the organization's success are evident at all levels. Intrinsic goals are also important.
Adversarial relationships abound. "We-they" mentality prevails, with a focus on grievances.	Labor-Management Relations	Relationship is simultaneously cooperative and adversarial. A variety of approaches are used to resolve differences with each party focused on the success of the business.
Good engineering, good machines, good materials; focus on output and numbers.	Key Factors for Success	Excellent quality, excellent service, committed employees; focus on quality of life processes and improvement.

philosophy from the traditional approach requires a re-view, and most likely a revision, of the organization's mission, vision, and values.

The organization must also rethink its structure and how it affects the organization's performance. Restructuring may not be needed in order to change, but a shift must definitely occur in how various components relate to one another. The structure will need to be looked at in three areas.

Vertical Structure. The organization will need to adjust its hierarchy not only in number of levels (fewer) but also in the roles of the various levels. The change should be in the direction of more equitable distribution of power and authority as well as on having the right levels doing the right things.

Horizontal Structure. The functional groups will need to be rethought in terms of better integration, customer focus, and cooperation. The focus should be on role clarification and integration and on improving relationships among specialists in achieving the *organization's* goals, not people's personal or area goals.

Team Structure. The organization will have to adjust itself to teams—not just at the first level, but throughout the entire organization. The aims include defining teams, identifying key goals and performance indicators, and developing team processes that support overall success.

Changes in structure must be accompanied by shifts in roles. Without role changes, the team-based process has little chance of success. A vertical shift results in a clearer definition of the roles in the three major levels of the organization: strategic (the top level does strategy planning and resource acquisition/allocation), management (the middle level is responsible for translating the overall strategy into reality), and implementation (the first level is responsible for day-to-day operations). A horizontal shift transforms the organization from one in which control is maintained through control of resources, information, or expertise to one characterized by cooperation and mutual support to achieve common goals.

Methods of operation must also change. More open, participative processes will be required for such things as budgeting, communication, and business strategies. A shift to a high-performance structure usually leads to a redefinition of work-related activities including jobs (probably a move toward more generic definitions), problem solving (more involvement at the lower levels of the organization), and business information (more relevant, timely information at the lower levels of the organization).

As an organization transforms itself from traditional to high performance, relationships change along various organizational boundaries. These boundaries include the vertical (between levels in the hierarchy), the horizontal (between departments or functional groups), union-management (less adversarial, more cooperative), and the external (suppliers, customers, corporate).

The Influence of Paradigms

An organization's paradigm, or particular view of reality, influences and guides how work is organized, how people are managed, how individuals and groups communicate, how labor and management relate, and so forth. Understanding the current paradigms of your organization is critical to the process of change.

Organizations have many reasons for doing what they do. The hard part is understanding why they continue on a particular course in the face of evidence that things are not working as well as they should.

In *Happy Are the Merciful*, Andrew Greeley (1992) portrays his character Terry Scanlan as deeply mired in the "previous paradigm." Greeley observes, "We can't live without paradigms because they organize reality for us…. We often cannot give them up even when we want to." The term *paradigm*, which comes from the Greek word for "pattern," was used by Thomas Kuhn in *The Structure of Scientific Revolutions* (1984) to describe a conceptual framework shared by a community of scientists. This framework defines the kinds of concerns (problems) on which the community should work and offers model solutions to these problems. Others since Kuhn have broadened the concept of paradigm to mean "the totality of thoughts, perceptions, and values that forms a particular vision of reality, a vision that is the basis of the way a society organizes itself" (Fritjof Capra in *Uncommon Wisdom*, 1989, p. 22).

Increasingly in the 1990s, the concept of paradigm has been applied to the operation of organizations. In this case, paradigms are seen as guiding how work is organized, how people are managed, how people communicate, how labor and management relate, and so on. Paradigms are part of the glue that holds the organization in place and ensures the stability of the organization over time.

The problem is that paradigms eventually outlive their usefulness. As Joel Barker indicates in *The Business of Paradigms* (1991), what was successful at one stage in the life of a product or organization will not necessarily be successful at the next stage of development.

The first step in changing paradigms is to recognize and understand the elements of the current paradigms. The exercise in Figure 1-2 will help you begin this process in your organization.

In the chart below list what you believe are the elements of your organization's current operating paradigm.

The Organization	Characteristics of the Current Paradigm
Who has power and authority?	
How do we communicate with employees?	
How does management listen to employees?	
How do we motivate employees?	
How do we view relationships between departments?	
How do we view and relate to employees?	
How do we view labor- or employee-management relations?	
Other	

Figure 1-2. Assessing Organizational Culture

Why Organizations Behave As They Do

Systems (organizations) are characterized by cycles
of events that are repeated over time. These cycles
tend to confirm what the organization is, how it ought
to operate, and what determines success. An organizational behavior model helps explain what supports
and reinforces existing paradigms and culture.

Let's get back to the question, "Why do organizations
continue to behave as they do even in the face of evidence
that the behavior is ineffective or destructive?" Why, for
example, would the top management of a company that
is losing money spend almost a million dollars for new
equipment when existing equipment could be repaired
and rebuilt for a third of that amount? Why would an
organization leave a manager in place whose area has a
terrible record of productivity and labor relations when
improvement of perfomance in that area is critical to the
success of the operation? Entrenched organizational paradigms are to blame. Here we introduce a behavior model
that shows how existing paradigms and culture are supported and reinforced.

Figure 1-3 shows the cycle of events in the model. They
are described below.

A. Condition or Event

Something triggers the cycle. It could be an action such as
a decision by a top manager or a grievance by a union
representative. Or, it could be an event such as the annual
budget preparation, the merit evaluation process, or the
opening of contract negotiations.

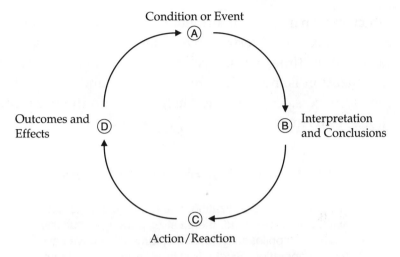

Figure 1-3. Organizational Behavior

B. Interpretation and Conclusions

Once an event occurs or an evaluation takes place, individuals process the experience, interpret the event (give meaning to it in their terms), and draw conclusions.

C. Action/Reaction

At the next step a person or group takes action or reacts. This may be a physical action such as preparing a budget, filling out a performance evaluation form, or responding to a grievance. Or the action may be in the form of thoughts that affect the person's emotions or attitudes.

D. Outcomes and Effects

Fourth, the person's or group's behavior has an outcome and affects the organization. For example, the department's budget is approved, the annual raise or bonus is awarded, or the grievance is settled.

This cycle creates a reinforcing loop as the outcome of one event becomes the basis for another event or action, which in turn triggers or influences the next action or event. Systems are characterized by cycles—events that are repeated over time. These cycles tend to confirm what the organization is, how it ought to operate, and what determines success. In short, they help maintain the organization's status quo.

Traditional Approaches to Change

To change an organization, one must be able to deal with, and understand, the existing paradigm, culture, leadership philosophy, and other forces that drive day-to-day operation. Single, traditional approaches to organizational change usually do not address the breadth or depth of elements involved in an organization's functioning.

In planning organizational change, one must keep in mind that *everything is connected to everything else*. One part of the organization cannot be altered in a substantive way without affecting and being affected by all the other parts.

Organizations have tried to initiate change in many ways. Some methods are successful, but when it comes to established, complex situations, most are not. Here are some traditional approaches to effecting change.

Legislate. Someone at the top says things will be different. The relationship between the person at the top and those who do the work will determine whether or not this approach works. Employees in complex organizations often do not respond to dictums when they do not (1) know the dictator, (2) like the dictator, or (3) believe the dictator is trustworthy.

Communicate. A leader says, "Gee, if workers just understood the problem, they are surely intelligent and rational enough to behave differently." So the organization publishes newsletters, makes videotapes, and holds meetings. However, an ongoing lack of understanding, trust, and credibility remove any chance that a standalone communication strategy will work.

Educate. Training can provide all sorts of interesting information, but it often has nothing to do with the real world; training does not change anything if issues rooted in culture and attitudes are left unaddressed. You can train all you want, but if you send managers and workers back into the same old culture and context, the effects of the training effort will evaporate immediately.

Participate. Participation was the strategy of the eighties. The Japanese were successful with it, so we should do it. Unfortunately, quality circles and problem-solving teams have often been viewed as strategies to get ideas from people and make them work harder for nothing in return. Participation without substantive change in power, cooperation, motivation, and communication systems is wasted effort in the long run.

Abdicate. "I can't run an organization full of crazy, lazy people." Many dabble in change efforts, then give up. When all else fails, as a last resort leaders abdicate the throne of change and go back to doing things the old way.

To gain some insights about your organization's attempts to change, complete the exercise in Figure 1-4.

Directions: To identify various efforts to change your organization during the last ten years and to evaluate the effectiveness of those efforts,
fill in the following chart. You can do so individually or as a group
(steering committee, management team).

Column 1—The Change Strategy. List all formal efforts to change (or
improve) the organization in the last five to ten years (e. g. , statistical
process control, first-line supervisor training, plant information meetings, etc.).

Column 2—Effectiveness Rating. Using the following scale, rate the effectiveness of each strategy.

1 = totally ineffective

2 = slightly effective

3 = moderately effective

4 = reasonably effective

5 = extremely effective

Column 3—Reasons for Success or Lack of It. Identify the reasons for
your effectiveness rating. Try to indicate what made the strategy effective or not.

**Evaluating Efforts to Change or Improve the Organization
in the Last Decade**

The Change Strategy	Effectiveness Rating	Reasons for Success/Lack of It
	1 2 3 4 5	
	1 2 3 4 5	
	1 2 3 4 5	
	1 2 3 4 5	
	1 2 3 4 5	
	1 2 3 4 5	
	1 2 3 4 5	

Figure 1-4. History of Change in Your Organization

The Conceptual Basis of Change

Change is driven by two key elements: pressure on the old culture and norms of an organization, and learning experiences that facilitate a paradigm shift from old theories and practices to new ones.

Change is a punctuated process, not a linear one. It is an evolving set of principles and practices that help organizations develop and learn to adapt over time. At the beginning of this process, what the organizational leadership usually wants to see and what they more often get are drastically different (see Figure 1-5). But as time goes on, a series of jumps ("Ahas!") occur in certain critical segments of the leadership. At these times, windows of opportunity emerge during which certain substantive changes are possible.

The human resource manager in a small manufacturing plant showed the plant manager an advertisement to recruit hourly workers that the plant was going to run in local papers. It was ready to go to the printer.

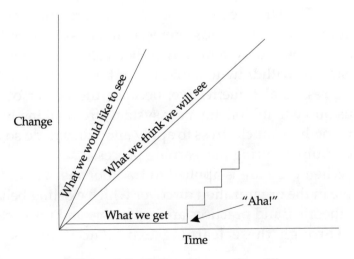

Figure 1-5. Change Process Over Time

Suddenly, the plant manager asked, "Isn't this the ad we used three years ago to recruit replacement workers during the strike?" It was the same one.

The plant manager suggested a meeting with the union president to see if the ad might cause a problem. Sure enough, the union president confirmed that publishing this advertisement would cause havoc throughtout the plant. Not only were there deep scars from the long, brutal strike, he said, but also, the plant was just settling down from the recent termination for theft of two employees. The ad, the union president said, would confirm rumors that more firings were on the way.

As a result of the meeting, and with the union's help, a new ad was developed, and a plantwide communication effort explained the purpose of the ad (with copy included), as well as described the schedule of events related to it.

This example represents a shift in the decision making paradigm based on new filters (how well this impacts present workers), sharing power (what will the union think?), and collaborative planning.

Two key elements in the change process are *stress* and *learning*. The stress comes from putting pressure on the traditional organizational systems. If the stress is excessive, however, the old system may either collapse under the pressure or withdraw to avoid it. On the other hand, too little stress is also ineffective, because the power of the status quo will inhibit any new systems from taking hold. Knowing how much stress to apply and when to do so is a skill acquired during the learning process.

When pressure is applied to traditional systems, key people in the organization discover which existing behaviors, theories, and practices are ineffective and unsuccessful. Through these learning experiences, and some coaching, leaders begin to see the world through a new set of lenses.

A Strategy Model for the Change Process

> To effect significant, permanent change, an organization must change its cycles of behavior. It does so by applying pressure to the four key elements of the organizational behavior model: the participation process, communication, leadership/business team development, and resolution of workplace issues.

Changing paradigms and permanently altering behavior patterns require an effective, sustained strategy. The change model that is described here is based on four major principles.

1. The strategy must isolate and generate pressure (create imbalance) on the existing paradigm and on traditional ways of doing things that no longer work.

2. The strategy should define and operate consistently with theories, values, and behaviors envisioned for the organization of the future.

3. When implemented, the strategy should generate data about what works and does not work both in the existing organization and in the strategy to change it.

4. The strategy should include structures and processes to facilitate and encourage learning—that is, gaining insight from the experience that leads to permanent change.

The change strategy has four key components: (1) a participation process, (2) communication for change, (3)

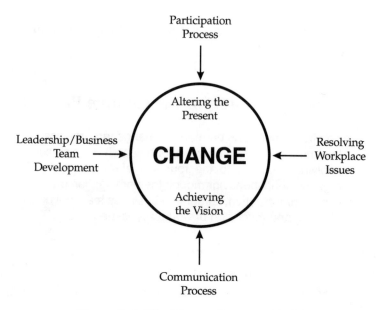

Figure 1-6. The Change Strategy Model

leadership/ business team development, and (4) resolution of workplace issues (see Figure 1-6).

The participation component is aimed at empowering employees through greater involvement in decision making and problem solving. The communication strategy both drives and reinforces the overall change effort. Leadership or business team development is aimed at creating high-performance teams among the leadership. And the issue-resolution component focuses on removing barriers to organizational growth and performance and on capturing major opportunities. Each of these elements is described in Chapter 4.

These strategic change elements apply pressure to the four corners of the organizational behavior model described in the following section, thus affecting the cycles of behavior within the organization. This process begins to transform the organization toward its desired state.

How to Influence Change in Organizational Behavior

Although events, people's perceptions and behaviors, and outcomes cannot be changed, mediating factors in organizational behavior can be influenced to help alter individual paradigms and behaviors. These mediating factors include perceptual filters, knowledge and skills, organization context, and feedback loops.

It is obvious that some aspects of the organizational behavior model we described in "Why Organizations Behave as They Do" cannot be changed. We cannot change events, peoples' perceptions, their actions/reactions, or outcomes. We can only influence the mediating factors of organizational behavior. These mediating factors have been added to the change strategy model in Figure 1-7. These four factors are perceptual filters, knowledge and skills, organization context, and feedback loops.

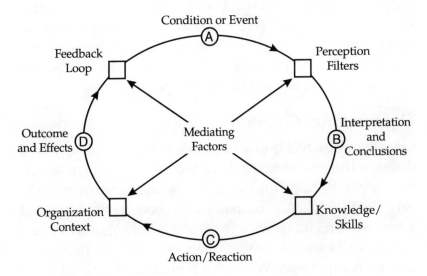

Figure 1-7. Mediating Factors in Organizational Behavior

Perceptual Filters

Each of us has a set of filters (visual, auditory, attitudinal, and so on), acquired through a lifetime of experience, that help us give meaning to events and data. For example, when we look at a thermometer in Fahrenheit, we understand what it means when it indicates 32 degrees. This same process occurs when we see people in an organization behave in a certain way over a period of time. Our experiential filters are the "translators" of events that help us draw conclusions about what is going on around us. Members of organizations have significant perceptual filters built up over time.

Knowledge and Skills

A person can respond to a situation only in light of the knowledge or skills he or she possesses. For example, if you do not speak French and find yourself lost in Paris, you will probably resort to sign language or drawing pictures as a way to communicate. In organizations, when people or groups interpret an event and draw conclusions, they use their respective knowledge and skills to define the range of possible responses. People usually choose their best knowledge and skills, which typically correlate with what worked in the past.

Organization Context

Once someone reacts to a situation, that reaction is filtered through the organizational context, which in turn affects the outcome. Take, for example, the auto industry in the early 1980s. Most car companies had both a long history of adversarial relations with the United Auto Workers and a business disaster waiting to happen with the increasing foreign competition. When the companies began to try to tell the union's bargaining units that things were bad and that changes needed to be made, the most common reaction was, "They're lying," or "I wonder what they're up to now?" The context of deep mistrust that had built up over forty years affected all the communication coming from top management and made it virtually impossible to influence employees.

Feedback Loop

The feedback loop segment of the model contributes to the "organizational memory." It connects the events of the past to the events of the future. If the outcomes are positive, the organization is more likely to repeat the pattern. If, however, the outcomes are negative, the organization will tend to avoid the pattern (even if it is the right thing to do).

For example, if a plant manager holds information meetings with employees and the outcome of those meetings is positive (people are interested and attentive, ask good questions, and express appreciation for the opportunity to attend), there is an increased probability that such meetings will be held in the future. If, on the other hand, employees are rowdy, bored, hostile, or abusive, it is less likely that such meetings will be held in the future. From another perspective, if the meetings are boring or if the presenters do not seem completely honest, employees are not likely to want to attend or to pay attention in the future. A good experience produces just the opposite response for presenters and attendees.

From Theory to Practice: Planning and Implementing Organizational Change

This chapter has introduced a model of organizational behavior and a basic strategy for change. The remainder of the book translates this theory into a practical

approach for implementing and managing change in
organizations.

This chapter has contrasted the characteristics of traditional organizations with those of high-performance organizations. It has also provided a theory of why
organizations stay the way they are and has offered a
model and strategy for beginning to change traditional
organizations. This section sets the stage for moving from
theory to practice in the change process.

The models described in this chapter are based on
many years of organizational and human research and
have served us well in the study of organizations and
organizational transformation. What is clear from the practice of managing transformation is that organizations cannot just wish themselves a new culture, nor can they
institute quick fixes to change years of practice. The alternative is a long, slow process that involves stressing the
organization, modeling the future, and learning from con-
trasting old practices with new efforts.

The process described in this book uses a parallel
structure to design and manage organizational transformation as well as to learn from the process of changing. The
change strategy includes involvement efforts, leadership
development, communication strategies, and special issues and interests.

The book moves from structure to design to implementation to managing change to barriers to learning. The
appendixes address private versus public sector change
and change in a unionized environment.

2

PLANNING FOR THE CHANGE PROCESS

General Framework for an Organizational Transformation Process

The model for change involves three phases: (1) describing the current organization; (2) determining where the organization wants to be; and (3) designing a strategy and structure to get from where the organization is to where it wants to be.

The approach to organizational change described in the rest of this book follows three key phases that create the framework for structuring the change process. Before embarking on the actual process, it is important to understand these steps and to see where they fit in the overall strategy.

The first phase involves describing the current organization. Before an organization considers change, it must have an accurate and clear idea of its current state. Doing so establishes a basis for comparison to the desired organizational state. Later chapters present several diagnostic tools and approaches for developing a clear picture of the current organization.

The second phase involves determining where the organization wants to be—the desired state. This phase focuses on discussing the mission, vision, values, and behaviors the organization wants to pursue. A means for defining your future organization is presented in this chapter.

Once it has determined its current and desired states, the organization moves to the third phase (described in Chapters 3 and 4) and develops the structure and strategy that will help it begin to move from the present to the ideal. Figure 2-1 summarizes the three phases of the change process.

Organizations do not move easily or logically from the traditional, control-oriented paradigm to the paradigm of the high-performance system. Once established, however,

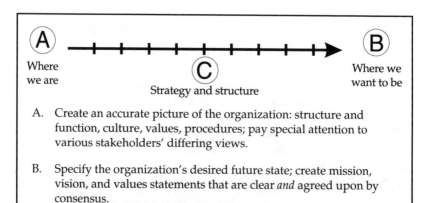

Figure 2-1. Framework for the Organizational Transformation Process

high-performance organizations create a continuous process of change over time as a way to adapt to new futures. The essence of this change process is in the organization's philosophy, roles, and procedures.

Planning Committee

> The planning committee makes the initial commitment to the team-based change process and designs the organizational steering committee structure. Its members consist of leaders representing key stakeholders.

The team-based change process begins with the establishment of a planning committee. This committee includes top management and, if the organization is unionized, top labor officials. Including labor and management on this committee begins to alter the boundary between the participants. Which top managers are included will depend on and affect the horizontal boundaries of the organization.

So committee makeup becomes a key factor in the change process.

The task of the planning committee is to design the organizational steering committee (change management structure) and to explore the process, consider benefits and liabilities, and make a firm commitment to proceed. This group helps think through the steering committee structures and the kinds of roles needed on the steering committee rather than identifying the individual people to be involved. The planning committee also helps design the strategy itself in terms of participation, management development, communication, and special issues to address. Figure 2-2 summarizes the makeup and tasks of the planning committee. Figure 2-3 is an exercise to help you determine the potential members of a planning committee for your organization.

The planning committee approach offers key stakeholders a chance to get their feet wet without actually going

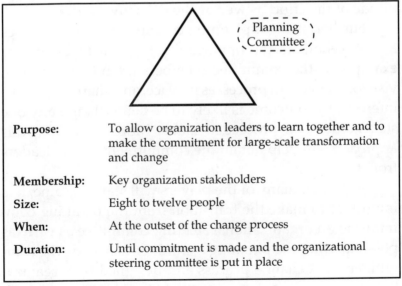

Purpose:	To allow organization leaders to learn together and to make the commitment for large-scale transformation and change
Membership:	Key organization stakeholders
Size:	Eight to twelve people
When:	At the outset of the change process
Duration:	Until commitment is made and the organizational steering committee is put in place

Figure 2-2. Planning Committee Summary

Identify the key roles and positions that ought to be part of a planning committee. Be sure to include the top manager, the chief human resources officer, and the top union leaders (if applicable). Beyond this core group, consider representatives of other key functions and stakeholders. A few examples are given.

Plant Manager _____   _____

Human Resources Manager _____   _____

Union President _____   _____

_____   _____

_____   _____

_____   _____

_____   _____

_____   _____

Figure 2-3. Planning Committee Membership

into the water. A major change effort represents a tremendous commitment—financial and professional—from the organization and its leadership. A planning committee gives this leadership the opportunity to consider the magnitude of the effort as well as the risks involved.

Further, using a planning committee approach gives key stakeholders the opportunity to learn together. For example, if the committee members attend conferences, visit locations with processes in place, and share respective interests, the outcome is likely to be better than if any one stakeholder had proceeded alone. More important, this approach will help obtain the commitment of key leaders from the outset.

Although many of the players will stay the same, it is important to make the transition from the planning committee to an organizational steering committee as early as possible. Once the planning committee has made the commitment to a change process and designed the organizational steering committee, it should be dissolved.

Motivation for Change

It is important for an organization to determine *why* it wants to change. The motivation for change can be positive (such as the desire to create a new kind of workplace) or negative (such as financial disaster). Understanding the conditions driving change in an organization is also important because they affect such things as the source and nature of commitment and the pace of the change process and the degree of persistence when the going gets tough.

A key question is: What is motivating the organization to change? Experience indicates that the most radical and quickest change occurs in organizations that are on the verge of going out of business. When the threat is great *and* when organizational members accept the reality of the threat, the organization is ready to do anything necessary to stay alive.

Of course, most organizations considering a change process are not at the point of disaster. Instead, they represent one of two conditions: (1) the organization is having trouble with productivity, quality, or employee relations (any of which can jeopardize the bottom line), or (2) the organization anticipates the need to be different and is looking for a process to encourage and support the change.

It is important to know what is motivating the need to change. Are there positive factors (such as the desire to create a new kind of workplace or the desire to improve quality) behind the effort? Or are the driving forces primarily negative (such as financial losses, labor trouble, loss of customers)? To understand the conditions driving change in your organization and to think about the implications, complete the exercise in Figure 2-4.

What are the primary motivators for change in your organization?

    Positive motivators: _____

    _____

    _____

    Negative motivators: _____

    _____

    _____

How are these factors likely to affect the design and implementation of the change process?

    In what areas are you likely to focus the change? _____

    _____

    _____

    How will these factors affect the pace of the change process? _____

    _____

    _____

Figure 2-4. Motivators for Change

The Diagnostic Process

The diagnostic process provides an understanding, or picture, of the organization from multiple perspectives through interviews, surveys, observation, and existing data. The diagnosis is normally performed by an external party, but the organizational steering committee plays a significant role. The diagnosis is the foundation for later discussion of the issues in, and strategy for, the change process.

Diagnosis helps describe the current organization. In the diagnostic phase, representatives from all levels of, and functions in, the organization are surveyed and interviewed. Employees are encouraged to talk openly about their workplace, its strengths and weaknesses. The result is a series of "pictures" of the organization as seen through the eyes of people in the various levels and functions. These pictures allow the organizational steering committee time to discuss and agree on the overall nature of the organization and the nature of specific work areas and levels. The diagnosis is the foundation for later discussion of the issues in, and strategy for, the change process.

In practical terms, the diagnosis serves four goals. First, it creates a common picture of the organization among key stakeholders (e.g., top management, functional managers, middle management, first-line supervisors, union leaders, work force constituencies). Second, it is one basis for developing a long-term plan and for evaluating the effort. Third, the diagnosis postures the transformation process as problem solving versus solution development. And finally, the diagnosis establishes initial credibility in the change process through accuracy of the picture, honesty about what the organization is and is not, and openness in talking about historical "undiscussables. "

The approach used in completing the diagnosis involves identifying the critical organizational variables and questions and creating the picture through interviews, survey, existing data, and observation. Logistical issues involve identifying the samples to be surveyed and interviewed by level, function, and position and actually conducting the survey process.

The organizational steering committee plays a significant role in the diagnostic process. The committee should be involved in planning the diagnosis with the consultant, overseeing the diagnostic process, interpreting the results, using the data in planning, and communicating the results and the subsequent plan to the work force. Under the guidance of an outside consultant, the entire work system and especially the steering committee can begin to agree on the current state of the organization.

If a change strategy is launched in a facility that has not done adequate diagnosis and planning, there is a risk of investing resources and crucial energy in a process the organization may not be ready to encourage and support. Without a common picture from which to plan, the committee members will tend to design solutions (strategies) for their own definitions of the problem.

The Role of Diagnosis in Organizational Change

Diagnosis should be treated as the first stage of a long-term change intervention. It serves three purposes: It is the entry into the organization; it is an opportunity to see how everything is connected to everything else; and it provides important data for planning.

A major concern at the diagnostic stage is that the organization will use the data to identify the troubled areas and go after them with a fervor, leaving untouched the elements of the culture that cause or contribute to the acute condition. What is the alternative? To treat the diagnosis as the first stage of a long-term change intervention. In a medical context, no one expects to be changed by a physical examination; similarly, the organization should not expect to be changed by the diagnosis.

As part of the transformation process, the diagnosis serves three critical purposes:

1. It is the entry into the organization. How the diagnosis is conducted, the accuracy of results, and willingness to "tell the truth" are the critical dimensions of the diagnostic process. If these are not done well, the next steps in the process can be

forgotten. The organization members will see this as just "one more program. "

2. It is a chance to see how everything is connected to everything else. If key people are able to view the larger picture in the data (the findings that step on their respective organizational "toes" are tough to take), they will see a pattern of authority, decision making, communication, competition, motivation structures, and labor relations, all tied together. No one area stands apart. Beginning to see the interconnectedness and the complexity of the situation is the first step in understanding the real nature of the challenge.

3. The diagnosis provides important data for planning. An initial question, for example, is what kind of participation strategy to use: problem-solving teams? business group teams? self-directed work teams? The diagnostic data provide some insights that will aid in making those decisions.

The steering committee is responsible for understanding and managing all of these possibilities. At the initial stage of the change process, the employees are only interested in whether those doing the diagnosis got it right and whether they will tell it straight. So it is important to pay special attention to this first step.

To help your organization think about the diagnostic process, we provide a series of planning questions in Figure 2-5. The planning committee can use these questions to develop an approach to understanding the organization.

Once the data have been collected and analyzed, those responsible for the diagnosis conduct a one- or two-day feedback session with the organizational steering committee. At this session findings are discussed, differences are

A. What are the key questions we need to ask to understand this organization?

Leadership style   Decision making
Interdepartmental cooperation   Communication
Problem solving   Reward and punishment
Labor/employee relations   Quality and productivity

B. How will we ask the questions?

Existing data   Focus groups
Interviews   Surveys

C. Who will ask the questions (or develop the survey)?

Outside consultants
Internal staff

D. Who will answer the questions?

Numbers of people
From what areas
With what roles

E. How will we analyze and interpret results?

To see the interconnections
To obtain all perspectives

F. How will we communicate results to the workplace?

Vehicle:
    In writing
    In person
Tone:
    Tell it straight
    Got it right

G. How will we use the results in planning?

To go after systems changes
To develop a workable strategy and structure for the change
    process
To identify "hot topics"

Figure 2-5. Structuring the Diagnostic Process

aired, and conclusions are drawn. From this session comes the picture communicated to the work force and the plan for the change process. Figure 2-6 provides an outline for an analysis and feedback session that culminates the diagnostic process.

Alternatives to Conducting a Diagnosis

An organization does not always have the time or resources or, in some cases, the need to conduct an in-depth survey and interview process. Because the diagnosis is critical to the change process, the organizational steering committee can select from such alternatives as focus groups, a diagnostic task force, and a large-scale data collection event.

The previous sections assumed that the most thorough and accurate picture of the organization is obtained through an in-depth interview and survey process. Such a process also represents the initial stage of the intervention and is key to getting to the next steps. Sometimes, however, an organization does not have the time or resources to conduct a comprehensive diagnosis. This section explores some alternatives.

The use of *focus groups* emerged in the 1980s. Focus groups typically consist of ten to fifteen people (in this case, employees or vendors or customers) who are interviewed about the organization (or product or service). Sometimes the interviews are taped for review by the person or people conducting the diagnosis. In cases of a transformation process we do not recommend taping because issues of trust and honesty are so important.

The advantage of focus groups is that they provide a fairly broad picture and are relatively accurate. They give more depth and "texture" than a survey process alone.

Once the diagnostic data have been collected and analyzed, the organizational steering committee should invest at least a day in hearing and understanding the emerging picture. The following is an outline for the conduct of such a feedback session.

I. Goals of the Diagnosis

    A. To create a common picture of the organization among key stakeholders

    B. To establish a baseline for

        1. Long-term planning

        2. Assessment of progress

    C. To posture the change process as problem solving as opposed to solution development

    D. To legitimize the change process (create credibility) by being accurate, honest, and open in the diagnostic process

II. Agenda for the Day

    A. Overview of the diagnostic process

    B. The picture of the organization

        1. Results of data collection and analysis

        2. Discussion

    C. Conclusions

    D. Critical issues and implications for the change process

III. Committee's Role in the Day

    A. Is to

        1. Listen/be open

        2. Verify/adjust

        3. "Learn"

        4. "See" a new picture

    B. Is *not* to

        1. "Fix" what is wrong (rather than understand culture and patterns)

        2. Focus strictly on problem areas and people (rather than the larger picture)

Figure 2-6. Diagnostic Analysis and Feedback Session Outline

They do not, however, provide the depth of information gained in individual and small-group interviews. In addition, some people will avoid putting tough issues on the table—even when the focus group consists only of peers— for fear of repercussions.

A second alternative is to use the organization's prior survey and interview activities. Often, historical data have not been integrated or utilized. A *diagnostic task force* can be organized to work with these existing data. The membership is voluntary, consisting of employees nominated by the members of the organizational steering committee. The steering committee gives the task force access to *all* results of previous surveys and interviews. The task force analyzes the data, develops interpretations, and writes a set of conclusions. The task force should also recommend how to disseminate results to the rest of the organization.

A third alternative is to conduct a large-scale *diagnostic event* as the strategy or as part of the entry into a long-term process. Such an event may include 75 to 400 people for one, two, or three days. Some of the activities in this event create data for a diagnostic picture of the organization and provide a sense of the critical issues. Although such events provide logistical challenges in the collection of data, they do yield a broad picture very quickly and might be an appropriate strategy for certain organizations.

Figure 2-7 provides a tool for determining which diagnostic method would work best for your organization.

Defining Your Desired Organization

To establish a foundation for designing the organization of the future, the mission, vision, and values must be clearly established. The mission is the purpose of the organization—its function in the larger society. The vision is what that organization will look like and how

Given the alternatives for creating an accurate picture of the organization, list the data available from previous efforts, then analyze the pros and cons of the diagnostic options.			
Diagnostic Approach	Data Available From Previous Efforts	Pros	Cons
Paper-and-pencil survey			
Small-group (4 or 5 people) interviews (peers)			
Focus groups (10–15 people)			
Analysis of existing data			
Large-scale (75–400 people) diagnostic event			

Figure 2-7. Deciding on a Diagnostic Strategy

it will operate. The values are what the organization stands for—the principles that drive the operation.

The change process requires a solid foundation for designing the organization of the future. This foundation consists of the mission, vision, and values desired in the organization. To be useful, these three elements must be clearly described and shared by the organization.

An organization's *mission* is a statement of the reason or reasons for its existence. It encompasses the ultimate purpose of the organization and the boundaries within which it operates.

Vision describes the desired future state or condition of the organization in terms of its outcomes, characteristics, and functioning. A vision should focus on strategic advantages, consider how the company adds value to others, and be clear enough to be used for making decisions.

Values are what the organization stands for and believes in. Values reflect the organizational culture and influence ways of thinking, believing, and acting. Think of values as guiding the way organizational members behave toward each other and approach their work.

Figure 2-8 provides the means for developing or clarifying the mission, vision, and values of your future

Framework	Who:	Planning committee
	When:	During and/or following the diagnosis
	Purpose:	To create the definition of the organization of the future.
Mission		Begin by listing the key concepts that should be included in your mission. Key concepts should respond to the following questions:
		1. What is the ultimate purpose for your existence?
		2. What is your ultimate aim?
		Brainstorm a list of phrases or sentences that describe your view of the ultimate purpose of your business. Be sure the list contains statements appropriate to the mission—eliminate goals and values statements.
		Once you have settled on the key elements (statements) for the mission, draft a summary consensus statement. Keep the mission as brief as possible (some writers recommend twenty-five words or less). In general, the more words you have, the less clear the mission.
Vision		Here is one approach to developing a vision statement:
		Have the planning committee envision itself giving a tour of the organization (or conversing with someone writing an article about it) three years in the future.

Figure 2-8. Determining Mission, Vision, and Values

Now, brainstorm a list of statements that reflect what the committee would like to say about the organization (e. g. , "We have the best quality in the country" or "Last year we had no lost-time accidents").

When you finish the list, you have the operational definition of your vision. Now you can either clean up the list and use it as your vision, or write a statement that summarizes the list.

The vision should stretch the organization beyond where it is, yet be something the organizational steering committee believes is achievable. If it is too close to the present, it does not drive the organization. If it is too unrealistic, it provides no motivation. The aim is to hit the middle ground.

Organizations often write vision statements that reflect common errors:

1. The mission and the vision cannot be distinguished.

2. The vision is so vague that few get meaning from it.

3. The vision is so far removed from present reality, nobody believes you can get there.

Resist the temptation to create a vision statement with which employees cannot identify.

Values   Go to the list the committee brainstormed (the tour or magazine article) for the vision. Read through it. Are there explicit value statements among the list (e. g. , "We value our people as much as our product")? Are there implicit value statements among the items on the list (e. g. , quality is more important than quantity; mutual trust and respect are the basis for the relationship between management and labor)? If you pull out the explicit value statements from the list and translate the implicit values into explicit statements, you have the organization's values.

In addition, the committee can brainstorm statements that represent fundamental principles of the organization (e. g. , "We believe in taking risks to achieve new levels of performance"). These statements, in addition to those discovered in the vision, provide a basis for the organization's values statements.

Figure 2-8. Determining Mission, Vision, and Values (continued)

organization. The products of this effort serve as the basis for design and decision making later in the process and in the operation of the organization.

Anticipating Resistance to Change

Although mission, vision, and values are critical to defining the future of the organization, the forces of resistance that stand in the way of change must also be recognized. Once these sources are assessed, they can be incorporated into the planning process.

Beyond identification of the current state of the organization and the vision for the future is the need to assess the potential resistance to change. This analysis is useful in the planning process and prepares the organizational steering committee and others for the slowness, disappointment, and frustration that are bound to occur. Assessment of resistance can be organized on two dimensions, as shown in Table 2-1: (1) whether it is external or internal to the organization, and (2) whether it can be influenced or controlled by the organization.

Table 2-1. Dimensions of Resistance to Change

Can the Organization Influence or Control?	Source of the Resistance	
	External	*Internal*
Yes	These factors should be incorporated into the business strategy.	These factors should be key targets for the organizational change strategy.
No	Try to minimize the impact of the resistance on the process.	Make the resistance visible; try to work with it; regularly review its impact on the process.

External sources of resistance include economic elements (e.g., interest rates), social factors (e.g., changes in work force characteristics), and political forces (e.g., legislation removing surcharges from imports). Internal sources of resistance include values (e.g., the new company president's commitment to the environment or a concern about keeping people employed in spite of shifts in the marketplace), leadership (e.g., the personality of a general manager), rewards (e.g., the nature of the organization's performance appraisal and bonus system), and protection of "turf" (e.g., who owns what in the organizational power hierarchy).

Figure 2-9 is an exercise to help you categorize the internal and external sources of resistance that are likely to operate on your organization and the transformation process. Identifying the sources of resistance will help you develop a picture of what is in the way of changing the organization and help you understand and deal with these forces. You are asked to list the five strongest internal and external sources of resistance to moving toward your organization's vision. After you have listed these sources: (1) indicate whether the source of resistance is controllable (or influenceable) by the organization and (2) rate each on the power scale at the bottom according to its relative strength. You can then plug the results into the planning process for the transformation process.

A. External Sources of Resistance

		Strength Rating	Controllable (Yes or No)
1.	_____	_____	_____
2.	_____	_____	_____
3.	_____	_____	_____
4.	_____	_____	_____
5.	_____	_____	_____

B. Internal Sources of Resistance

		Strength Rating	Controllable (Yes or No)
1.	_____	_____	_____
2.	_____	_____	_____
3.	_____	_____	_____
4.	_____	_____	_____
5.	_____	_____	_____

Strength of Resistance

Very Weak		Weak		Medium Strength		Strong		Very Strong
1	2	3	4	5	6	7	8	9

Figure 2-9. Resistance Analysis

3

STRUCTURE FOR THE CHANGE PROCESS

Change Management Structure

When change strategies are implemented within an existing organization, an attempt may be made to isolate, reject, or co-opt the process. A "parallel" change structure can be created to counteract the organization's tendency to preserve the status quo. The purpose of this parallel structure is to give the organizational members a place to design and manage the change process. As a model for the organization of the future, this structure of committees brings people together in ways different from the current organization and asks them to behave in different ways. (An alternative to the parallel change management structure is to make the business units responsible for the process. See Chapter 3, Business Unit Steering Committees, for an explanation.)

One way to support the change strategy is to create a parallel structure—an organizational framework built alongside the existing organization within which the change process is actually designed and managed (see Figure 3-1). The framework consists of steering committees, adjunct committees, task forces, and work/business teams.

One of the most important tasks of formal organizational structure is maintaining the status quo. Stability is achieved through and within the confines of the existing culture and paradigms. Because the existing structures are responsible for the maintenance of the status quo and because they tend to want to preserve themselves, people operating within the traditional structure will have great difficulty seeing what is wrong and what needs to happen to change it.

The parallel change structure is one way to overcome these limitations. Because it is created outside the current structure, the parallel change structure is not subjected to the day-to-day pressures, rules, and obligations of the

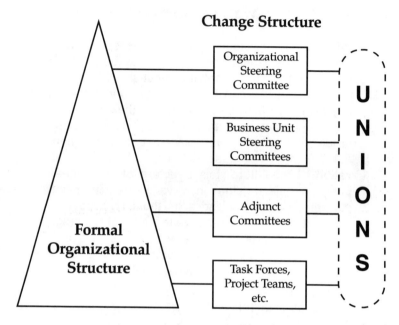

Figure 3-1. Organizational Structure and Change Structure

existing structure. This approach does two things: (1) it puts people together who are not otherwise in the same place (for example, union leaders are not part of management teams), and (2) it asks them to behave differently with each other and with the organization as a whole (for example, to conduct their business on the basis of a consensus model).

This change structure is linked horizontally to the business by correlating the organizational level of the committee with the membership. Selection of committee members is based on the principle that "who's there is what's likely to change." The organizational steering committee must contain the top manager and, if applicable, the leadership of the unions, because these leaders, more than anyone else, need to change. In addition, the committee should include key functional area leaders, the choice of whom determines the probable relationship changes that will occur.

Should there be a representative from every constituency involved in the change structure? Our answer is no! Here are some guidelines for *who* to involve *where:* (1) senior managers should be on the organizational steering committee, (2) functional line managers should be on the business unit steering committees, and (3) a mix of others who reflect the concerns and interests of all other stakeholders should participate at both levels. Complete representation usually means too many people, which bogs down the committee's ability to reach consensus. The committee members must be structured in such a way that everyone believes in the integrity of the effort and trusts what comes out of the committees.

Two problems are common to parallel structures that fail. First, they have not been designed in a real parallel relationship to the formal business structure, so that the change effort is not connected to the business. Second, the membership of committees is either based on the total representation model (vertical and horizontal slices) or, more commonly, is "manipulated" around key people (e.g., people who are likely to support the process are selected). The right people need to be included. The committee design should be based on what the company wants to be, not on what currently exists.

Organizational Steering Committee

The role of the organizational steering committee is to design (or refine) the change process and strategy and to monitor, evaluate, and adjust the change effort. The committee serves three roles in the change process: semidetached observer, decision maker, and change agent. Membership of the committee should be limited to twelve, and selection criteria should be followed rather than just choosing those who are likely to support the effort.

The organizational steering committee is a top-level, integrated, parallel structure made up of the leadership of key stakeholders (see Figure 3-2). It exists outside the formal organization hierarchy in order to include more stakeholders than traditional structures do and to keep the change process free of the rules and procedures of the status quo. At the same time, the members of the committee come from those formal hierarchies in order to create the tension for change and the opportunities to learn.

This steering committee serves as the executive unit of the change process. Its purposes are to design the overall process and strategy, to oversee the implementation and development of the process, and to encourage changes in the permanent organization based on learning from the change process. At the outset, the committee is responsible for specifying the mission of the process, developing a vision of what the organization will look like if the process is successful, and identifying the key values and beliefs that support the effort.

As the process is put into place, the organizational steering committee will play several roles. One is an *academic role*, that of semidetached observer. In this role the steering committee observes, collects, and shares data; analyzes what works and what doesn't; and tries to determine why. Second is the *control role:* serving as decision maker in the overall process. The committee decides what is required to get to the vision and is responsible for designing and managing the process. The third role is *change agent*. The committee ensures that the barriers to change are removed, the problems—not the symptoms—are corrected, and the successful

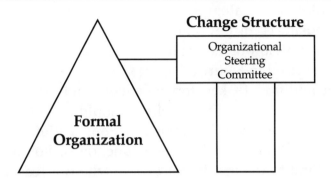

Change Structure

Organizational Steering Committee

Formal Organization

Purpose: To design, monitor, evaluate, and adjust the change process and strategy.

Membership: Leadership of key stakeholders in the organization. Some rotation acceptable.

Size: No more than twelve.

When: Formed as the first formal commitment to change.

Duration: Ongoing.

Role:

- Develop vision and goals for the change process in the organization as a whole or the respective area(s) for which it is responsible.

- Develop a cultural change strategy for the organization. This strategy may include participation strategies, leadership team development, communication vehicles and processes, and resolution of issues and constituents' concerns.

- Implement the cultural change strategy in the organization. The implementation plan may include orientations, training, skill development, and team launches.

- Coach, monitor, and evaluate the overall change process.

- Promote communication about change and the process in the organization.

- Coordinate and communicate about the activities of this committee with other areas, steering committees, or management groups.

- Model the behaviors of the new culture for the rest of the organization.

- Discuss and learn about the relationship between the day-to-day business and the change process and to move the day-to-day business toward the vision of the process.

Figure 3-2. Organizational Steering Committee Summary

principles and strategies are integrated into the "way of doing business" in the organization.

An overview of the organizational steering committee is summarized in Figure 3-2.

In addition to key top managers and labor representatives, the steering committee should include critical stakeholders at other levels or functions. Ultimately, the choice of whom to include is a function of holding the upper limit to the number of people who can reasonably do consensus decision making (normally a maximum of twelve). It is a mistake to base membership on including only the "good guys" (those who are expected to support the effort) or to include people because their constituency doesn't trust the organization's leadership (if they aren't there, they assume decision makers are not considering acting in their best interest). The key in the change process is to behave as a committee in a way that demonstrates concern for everyone's interests, thereby earning everyone's trust and respect.

The development of this committee is critical. It should be launched with a two- or three-day retreat. The retreat should include team building, conducting a general diagnostic activity, learning about change processes, and beginning to build a plan. The initial retreat is, however, only the first step in a long-term development process.

Business Unit Steering Committees

Business unit steering committees are also created alongside the existing organization structure. In organizations that have begun a transformation process, specifically in the form of integrated business units, it may be more reasonable to make these business units responsible for the change management process rather than creating a separate structure. One criterion, especially in organized workplaces, is whether union officials are part of the business unit. If not, then the parallel change management structure is recommended. The role of these committees is to develop goals for, and implement, the change process in the various business areas. Three key decisions must be made about the committees early in the process: organization, membership, and role/responsibility.

The next level of structure puts steering committees in place alongside the organization's key business units. The business unit steering committees are charged with implementing the overall strategy within the business structure. Questions must be answered in three areas with regard to establishing these committees.

Organizing the Committees

- Will there be a committee in each functional manager's area (e.g., manufacturing units, maintenance, finance, human resources, materials, etc.), or will the committees be organized around the core business units, with representatives from the functional areas that support each unit?

Membership of the Committees

- Will membership be horizontal (leadership/representation from the various functional areas in the unit) or vertical (a "slice" of the organization including, for example, representatives from each layer of the unit)?
- Will membership be voluntary? Will membership rotate? How often?

Committees' Role and Responsibility

- What is the role of the business unit committees versus the organizational steering committee?
- How do these committees interface with business decision making (management teams)? with labor/employee relations processes?
- How do the committees translate learning from the process into permanent organizational changes?
- What are the committees' roles and responsibilities with regard to administration and planning? solving problems in the organization? communicating? evaluating the process?

These issues are summarized in Figure 3-3.

Creating and sustaining the business unit committees is much harder and more complex than establishing the top-level organization committee. Early in the process the change structure will reflect the pathology of the existing organization. For example, it is not unusual to see power struggles between the organizational steering committee and business unit committees. The key point is, in this process participants have the license, time, and structure to put these issues on the table, to understand what drives them, and to find ways to work through them in a way not possible in the day-to-day business. The assumption is that if participants can work through the tough issues here, it will not only affect the daily operation of the organization but also provide the opportunity to develop the skills and courage to make permanent changes where necessary.

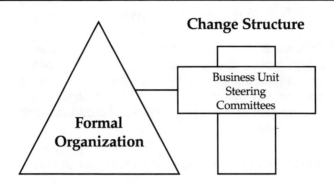

Purpose: To implement the change process at the business unit level.

Membership: Horizontal or vertical, depending on design. Rotation of membership, depending on design.

Size: No more than twelve.

When: Following formation of the organizational steering committee.

Duration: Ongoing.

Role:

- Develop goals for the change process in the respective area(s) for which it is responsible.
- Develop a cultural change strategy for the organization. The strategy may include task teams, problem-solving work groups, team meetings, management team development and other forms of employee involvement strategies.
- Implement the cultural change strategy in the organization. The implementation plan may include orientations, training, skill development, and team launches.
- Coach, monitor, and evaluate the change process.
- Promote communication about the change process in the organization.
- Coordinate and communicate about their activities with other areas or steering committees.
- Model the behaviors of the new culture to the rest of the organization.
- Discuss and learn the relationship between the day-to-day business and the change process.

Figure 3-3. Business Unit Steering Committees Summary

Adjunct Committees

As a result of the diagnostic process or as an organization moves through the change process, special issues arise that need to be addressed. These issues are handled by adjunct committees created by the organizational steering committee or the business unit committees.

Adjunct committees provide special focus in one of three ways.

1. They work on and oversee a special *area of the overall change process* (e.g., communication for change).

2. They work on a specific organizational *issue* (e.g., policy revision).

3. They represent a *constituency's* concerns or needs (e.g., a supervisors' task force).

The adjunct committees give breadth and depth to the change effort. They are created by, and are responsible to, either the organizational steering committee or a business unit committee. Adjunct committees can be permanent or temporary.

Permanent committees may interact with all steering committees in the course of doing business but are typically responsible to the organizational steering committee. Interim committees focus on a special topic or the needs of a specific constituency and are responsible to the organizational steering committee, the business unit steering committees, the constituency, or a management team. Temporary committees may last for as little as a month or for over a year. The understanding, at least at the outset, is that they are designed to address a specific issue or constituency and at some point will have fulfilled their purpose. Figure 3-4 contains examples of permanent and temporary committees that sometimes emerge in a change process.

Permanent Committees

Communication Committee

A communication committee is responsible for designing and overseeing communication processes and content to both reflect and drive the overall change process (see Chapter 5). Typically, a communication committee will analyze communication needs, evaluate existing vehicles and their effectiveness, and design tools and procedures to overcome limitations and fill gaps.

Training and Development Committee

If the organization has no formal training organization (or has one that does not provide the overall content and service required), a training and development committee can be charged with analyzing and monitoring training needs, developing or identifying resources to meet those needs, and evaluating the ongoing effectiveness of the training effort.

Labor-Management Forum

Sometimes labor-management relations require more attention than is possible in the integrated steering committee structure. Some organizations have established a labor-management forum consisting of labor relations staff, union officials, and managers. This forum is charged with exploring labor-management issues (some of which may fall into the collective bargaining arena) in a nonadversarial context, using the approaches and techniques acquired in the change process.

Temporary Committees

Food Service Task Force

Diagnosis may reveal widespread dissatisfaction with the company's food service. The organizational steering committee then creates a task force to study the situation, develop alternatives, and make a recommendation for the future. The task force is reconvened within a year to evaluate the changes made.

Figure 3-4. Examples of Adjunct Committees

Supervisors' Task Force

Probably one of the most overlooked and "underpowered" constituencies in American companies is first-line supervision. More and more organizations have seen fit to provide this group with special attention during the early stages of the transformation process. The assumption is that if supervision does not change, nothing changes. A supervisors' task force can be responsible for any or all of the following:

- Redefining the role of supervision
- Identifying supervisors' training and development needs for the future
- Identifying reward and recognition needs of supervision

Figure 3-4. Examples of Adjunct Committees (continued)

4

STRATEGY FOR THE CHANGE PROCESS

Design of the Change Strategy

The change strategy is developed by the organizational steering committee, based in part on information collected in the diagnostic process. The design of the change strategy addresses four elements: participation/team structure and development, leadership team development, communication and information systems, and resolution of organizational issues.

After the organizational steering committee is in place and has begun to function, and after the diagnostic phase is complete, the committee is ready to design the overall change strategy. This strategy is built around four areas: participation/team structure and development, leadership team development, communication and information systems, and resolution of organizational issues.

Although the design process generally begins with participation, all four elements can be designed simultaneously. For example, the diagnosis may suggest forming a communication committee early in the process or putting a particular task force in place immediately. The organizational steering committee should feel free to be flexible. The issue of what to do when should evolve as the organizational steering committee works through the early phases of start-up and reviews the diagnostic results.

A diagram of the influences on the design of the strategy is shown in Figure 4-1. The figure depicts how the mission and vision, diagnosis, motivators for change, and current state of the organization all affect the design. In Chapter 2, we discussed two influences on the design of the change strategy: the diagnostic process and development of the mission, vision, and values for the organization. In this chapter, we examine the other two influences: the status of the organization in relation to growth and decline, and motivation systems.

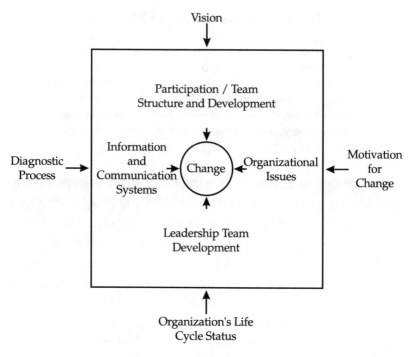

Figure 4-1. Change Strategy

The Organization's Life Cycle Status

It is important to spend time determining where the organization is and discussing appropriate steps for moving forward. Characterizing the organization's current status can be done using a life cycle model.

Organizations can be characterized in stages of growth and decline. Figure 4-2 shows a life cycle curve that has been applied to everything from product life cycles to organizational life cycles. It is useful because the various life cycle periods (stages) represent different activities and emphases in organizational functioning.

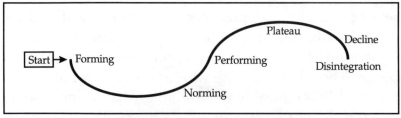

Figure 4-2. Life Cycle Curve

Forming period: Characterized by start-up, early organization, chaos, and rapid change.

Norming period: Characterized by the institutionalization of structure, procedures, functions, and norms.

Performing period: Characterized by continuous improvement and growth using the model and procedures developed during the norming stages. Changes are incremental and consistent with the determined direction.

Plateau period: Improvements begin to level off and stabilize. Growth ceases. Old structures and procedures for getting better do not seem to help "bend" the curve.

Decline period: The combined "gravity" of the status quo and the environment contribute to a period of decline.

Disintegration: If the trend in the decline period is not countered in a significant way, the organization may cease to exist.

The notion that "where you are determines where you can go" is based on the fact that each of these stages has its own set of principles and practices for improvement and for moving to the next stage. What is appropriate in the norming period is not necessarily appropriate in the plateau period. Therefore, knowing where you are in the organizational cycle is critical to determining what is appropriate to getting to the next stage (or improving within the current stage). Figure 4-3 provides an exercise for determining where your organization is on the life cycle curve.

If an organization is, for example, somewhere midway through the performing period, teams may have a different role and function than if the organization is on the verge of the decline period. In the performing stage, teams may be used to help solve problems related to improvement; in the

---

Here is an easy exercise for gathering data on perceptions of where your organization is on the life cycle curve. You can use the exercise with 10 people or 100. In fact, the more you have, the more likely you are to approximate the real state of the organization.

Step 1.   Explain the organizational life cycle curve to the participants.

Step 2.   Tell participants that the goal is to figure out where your organization is on the curve.

Step 3.   Get participants' assessments.

- If you have a small group (8–15) you could have them give you a rating verbally or mark the rating on a flip chart.

- If you are dealing with a larger group (20–100), you can put a drawing of the curve on a wall (use flip chart paper) and have each participant either put an "X" where he or she thinks the organization is or use a colored dot to paste up his or her position.

Step 4.   Interpret the results.

Step 5.   Have a discussion about what the profile means in terms of the strategy you use and the resistance you are likely to encounter.

Figure 4-3. Organizational Life Cycle Exercise

plateau or decline period, teams may be the key to inventing new products, opening new markets, or developing new processes that change the business radically.

The problem for an organization trying to change when it is in the plateau or decline period is that most individuals and existing structures tend to view the situation as just another "bleep" in the performing curve. This attitude occurs because organizational growth is never in a smooth, straight line. As a result, people who have been in the organization for a while have a set of perceptions that says, "Hey, this is just another temporary downturn; we'll come out of it just like before. " This thinking may be the single most threatening barrier you will encounter. For if these people are successful in convincing leadership that the experience is only a "bleep," by the time the truth is realized, it is often too late. Therefore, it is important to spend some time with the leadership of various stakeholders in the organization determining where you are and discussing what seems appropriate in moving forward.

Motivation and the Change Process

Organizational motivation systems are a powerful element of performance and change. The management of motivation issues occurs in three steps.

One of the key elements in designing and conducting the change process is consideration of the role of motivation. The management of motivation issues occurs in three steps.

Step 1.   Reduction of the punitive, negative systems and behaviors that are in the way of people moving toward the vision.

Step 2.   Revision of systems and procedures aimed at maintaining the old culture and the status quo.

Step 3.   Transformation of old, extrinsic motivation sys-
           tems and introduction of new, high-perform-
           ance systems and structures.

These steps are not necessarily discreet; that is, it is not
necessary that one be finished before the next one starts.
In fact, they probably overlap a great deal. Further, not
every organization will start at Step 1. Depending on the
current state of the organization and the work that pre-
ceded the process, it is possible to start at any phase.
Figure 4-4 lists some of the activities and areas of interest
in the respective steps.

Step 1

Reduce the Negative

Review and revise unnecessary and irrelevant punitive policies. Every
organization has numerous policies and rules that have been in place
forever. Almost no one remembers why they came about or what purpose they serve. Many probably resulted from behavior of one or a few
employees a long time ago and have long outlived their usefulness. Even
worse, punitive policies serve as constant reminders to the good employees of how management feels about them (and reinforce the self-fulfilling
prophecy syndrome).

Another way to reduce the negative is to clean up old labor agreement
language. Some new bargaining processes focus on taking out old negative language and/or converting it to positive wording.

Reinforce the Positive

Think and talk about ways to reinforce intrinsic motivation in the change
process. Many workplaces have instituted extrinsic motivators in the
form of hats, jackets, and so forth. Work on motivators that affect how
people feel, such as recognition processes (articles in the newsletter,
recognition at meetings, the opportunity to present proposals to top
executives, etc.). Also, if you really want a team-based organization,
figure out strategies to motivate teams, not individuals.

Figure 4-4. Examples of Activities in Managing Motivation Issues

---

Step 2

Look at Management Reward and Recognition Systems

Many organizations base annual merit bonuses or increases on a set of objectives written for the individual manager or supervisor. Every organization with which we have worked has eventually concluded that such systems lead to destructive competition and less-than-optimal outcomes for the overall business. Have the management team invent a new system for merit performance that is based on the success of the business as a whole, mutual goals, and support among related areas.

Step 3

Reduce the Negative

Review major motivation systems such as incentive programs. What are the assumptions on which they are based? What kind of behavior do they reinforce? How do they fit with the vision? Many worker incentive systems were developed in eras where productivity alone was king. Now, they get in the way of producing quality at the lowest possible cost.

Reinforce the Positive

Find ways to answer an entire work force's question "What's in it for me to change?" by developing reward and recognition systems that fit the vision. Increasingly, gain- and profit-sharing systems are a way to increase stakeholders' commitment. Be careful, however, about instituting such programs without sufficient forethought and planning.

Figure 4-4. Examples of Activities in Managing Motivation Issues (continued)

Exploring Team Strategy Options

Selecting the appropriate level of team participation is critical to the success of the change strategy. Planners have a wide range of options, from working with the traditional structure to team-based, high-involvement strategies.

Before your organization leaps on the participation horse and goes riding off in pursuit of the latest trend in employee involvement, stop a moment to ask the following critical question: Is our organization suited to a team-based strategy as the primary intervention? Believe it or not, some organizations will do better with a traditional structure and work group function than with high-involvement teams.

Here are some of the reasons you might *not* want to pursue a team-based strategy.

- The organization is not structured for, and will not support, teams.
- The work force has a lot of seniority and the majority of workers prefer to "do things the old way. "
- The nature of the work is not complex; there is a lot of turnover in the work force.

The vast majority of organizations will benefit from a team-based strategy, but it is worth exploring the question just to be certain you do not invest a lot of time and resources in an effort that is unnecessary or inappropriate.

The primary participation and team development effort requires a combination bottom up/top down strategy. Many pure team development efforts begin at the top and cascade down the layers of the organization. At the other extreme, many of the employee involvement efforts put teams in place at the bottom of the organization with no systematic effort to change the nature of structures/teams and leadership above. The model described here goes both directions more or less simultaneously.

We believe that the initial effort should be directed at the first level of the organization. This is where the talent and energy, left unnoticed for so long, is frozen. At the same time, as the organization begins to open up with a new kind of involvement and empowerment, the teams at this level will both pressure the upper levels to change and teach the organization something about what is possible in a team-based culture.

As first-level teams go into place, planners should give serious consideration to the management or business team strategy. This is where the organization's status quo is maintained. The first-level effort is futile unless two things are accomplished: (1) the nature of the management team tradition is put on the table and addressed, and (2) some new commitments and skills are put in place to allow management teams to behave differently with each other and with other teams in the future. A major weakness of the quality circle era was that organizations tended to view teams or circles as ends, not means. Leadership in organizations thought that with the creation of the teams and the installation of the program, the task was finished. The fact is that creation of teams is merely the first step in a fairly long journey of organizational change.

Figure 4-5 graphs various team and involvement options based on the depth of involvement in the business and the length of time the participation option is in place.

Selecting the Team-Based Strategy

The choice of team-based strategy depends on two key factors: the vision of the future organization and the maturity of the current organization. The types of team options available fall along a continuum and vary in terms of membership, function, life span, leadership, and participation. Many approaches to team leadership must also be considered.

Designing a team strategy involves more than just looking at the various options available (total quality teams, sociotechnical systems, self-managing work teams,

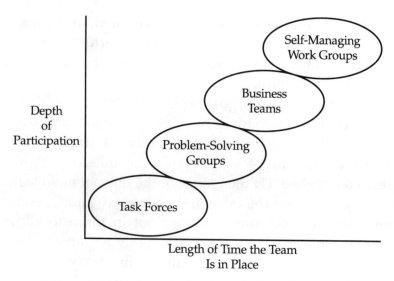

Figure 4-5. Team Strategies in Employee Involvement

etc.) and choosing the one you think is best. Rather, the team-based strategy is a product of two key factors:

$$\frac{Team\text{-}based}{Strategy} = \frac{Vision\ for\ the}{Organization} \times \frac{Maturity\ of\ the}{Organization}$$

The vision is critical. It defines what the organization wants to be and how planners want it to operate. Without the vision, one has no guiding principles for designing and implementing the team-based strategy. If the vision is only incrementally different from the organization's current status, one would probably not choose a radically different team model for the organization (e.g., self-directed teams). On the other hand, if the future vision includes a flatter organizational structure and fewer managers and supervisors doing traditional supervision, choosing a low-involvement approach such as problem-solving teams is probably not going to get the desired results. In this case, business teams or self-directed work groups would be a better choice.

The second consideration is the maturity of the organization. Maturity includes both the extent to which management, staff, and supervision are willing to redefine territories and power and the extent to which the frontline work force can and will accept responsibility in a new way. If the organization has limitations in either area, high involvement becomes more difficult. If there are limitations in both areas, serious thought should be given to a strategy that will help both entities mature before launching into more significant team strategies. In such a case, the early approach might be task forces or problem-solving groups with a plan to transition to business teams (see Table 4-1).

The challenge is creating a strategy between the extremes of one that does not stress the status quo and one that is so radically different from the existing operation that

Table 4-1. Team Strategies in Relation to
Organizational Vision and Maturity

Maturity of the Organization	Extent of Change in the Vision	
	Incremental	Significant
Low	Task forces and problem-solving teams as the permanent strategy	Low or moderate involvement strategy as the first step in a developmental process
High	Moderate involvement strategy, such as business team meetings and critical performance-related task forces	Move as quickly as possible to high-involvement strategies, such as business teams or self-managing work teams

people cannot connect and get involved. The decision ultimately requires good data and good intuition.

Team Options

There are only a certain number of true variations for team-based strategies. Table 4-2 presents a comparison of the four main options on the dimensions of membership, function, life span, leadership, and participation. Keep in mind, however, that there is no definitive break between these types of teams. Rather, they should be viewed as an overlapping set of options on a continuum.

The team planning process must address the strategy for the present with a view toward the future. If, for example, the long-term vision is for an organization characterized by high-involvement, self-sufficient teams but the current organization is not at all ready to commit to that extent, the transformation process might start with problem-solving groups and evolve to business teams and eventually implement self-directed work groups.

Again, we want to emphasize that the planning process for teams is more like inventing an organization for the future (or rather a strategy on how to get there) than a shopping expedition for the right team strategy. You must be prepared to spend more time designing the future of the human system than you would designing a new manufacturing or health care system. The human system is far more important and a whole lot harder.

Team Leadership Options

A number of team-based strategies make assumptions about the nature of team leadership and the extent of leader involvement in activities. At one extreme is the model that assumes the team's manager or supervisor must lead all team activities. At the other extreme is a democratic model

Table 4-2. A Comparison of Various Types of Participative Teams

Team Element	Team Type			
	Task Force	Problem-Solving Group	Business Team	Self-Managing Work Group
Membership	Within a department or between departments[1]	Within a department or between departments[2,3]	Supervisor and crew/team[4]	Natural work group + support personnel + resource consultants
Function	Resolve a specific issue or complete a specific task	Problem-solve: • Brainstorm • Select issues • Resolve issues • Recommend solutions	Weekly/biweekly meeting: • Information • Listening • Problem solving	Set goals Organize work Manage business
Life span	Time bound and/or task bound	As long as they wish; more than one year is typical	Permanent	Permanent
Leadership	Elected/appointed	Supervisor, union leader, and/or team member[5]	Supervisor and others as appropriate	Natural work group leader
Participation	Voluntary	Voluntary	Mandatory[6]	Mandatory

Notes: [1]Membership is typically voluntary but may be appointed.
[2]Membership is typically voluntary.
[3]Predominately made up of permanent members but may use temporary members or resource persons as needed.
[4]Will include others (e.g., resource or support people) on temporary or semipermanent basis as needed.
[5]Leaders/facilitators may be elected or appointed.
[6]May be voluntary depending on the nature of the work, workplace, history, etc.

that says the team should elect its leadership for activities such as team meetings or problem-solving sessions.

Either approach could be appropriate for your organization, or you might choose a combination of styles based, again, on where the organization is (maturity) and where you want it to go (vision). Here are the major options.

- *Supervisor/manager leads all activities.* This approach simply adds the new duties of the team strategy to the existing role of the manager or supervisor.

- *Team members are (s)elected to give leadership to some activities.* In this approach, team members are chosen to give leadership (sometimes in the form of facilitation) to team activities such as team meetings, task forces, or problem-solving sessions.

- *Supervisor/manager and team members divide the duties.* In this variation, the supervisor/manager assumes responsibility for some activities while team members take responsibility for others.

- *Supervisor/manager and team members share duties.* In this approach the supervisor or manager and a team member (usually elected by the team) function together to give leadership to activities. They share responsibility for organizing and conducting team meetings and cofacilitate activities such as problem solving.

Table 4-3 explains why the various options might or might not be a good idea for a given organization. We are not advocating a team strategy that turns the work team into a voting booth (the fear of many managers) or that condones the old culture under a new label. Somewhere between is an approach that both models the future and maintains the stability necessary for the effective operation of the business.

Table 4-3. *Comparison of Team Leadership Options*

Team Leadership Option	Why It Might Be a Good Idea	Why It Might Be a Bad Idea
Supervisor or manager leads all activities	Involvement activities are probably one of the few ways that managers or supervisors can practice new behaviors. Giving them responsibility for all activities is a major developmental opportunity. They must, however, be trained and coached over time if this option is to work.	The team will probably see this as another smokescreen for the same old stuff. This is especially true if the historical relationship between the team and supervisor has been strained. Also, if the organization is not prepared to provide training, monitoring, and coaching support, nothing may change.
Team elects leaders for various activities	This option was often seen in quality circles strategies. If the team elects their leadership, they feel more in control of the process and will tend to trust it more going in.	Teams may choose leaders out of an old model and not think about what is needed in the new context. Second, if not chosen as the leaders, supervisors often feel disenfranchised by such a strategy and will indirectly sabotage the effort or simply let it die on its own.
Supervisor and team members divide some team activity duties	This approach allows supervision to maintain control and to learn by being responsible for some activities while supporting team members gaining entry to the new work process by being responsible for others.	Dividing the activities prevents modeling of cooperation between team members and the leadership, and it is possible that either constituency may resent the division (for different reasons).
Supervisor and team members share some team activity duties	This approach gives the formal leadership a chance to learn by being responsible for the new activities. At the same time, it recognizes the overall responsibility of the manager or supervisor for the success of the team. In addition, the team gets a chance to assume more responsibility and to begin to provide internal leadership.	Problems can arise if the personalities of the coleaders do not mesh or if the manager or supervisor does not treat the team member as a partner in the coleadership relationship. Monitoring and coaching are essential if this approach is to work.

Testing the Team Strategy Before Implementing It

Once the organizational steering committee members have selected the participation/team strategy that seems to best fit the organization, the members should talk to the teams and supervisors before implementing their selection. Doing so models the values of the new process as well as helps with the decision about the team-based strategy. In the course of such discussions, the steering committee members often get feedback that allows them to make improvements in the plan.

The goal is to be sure that the chosen strategy fits the organization and the business units. To find out, the steering committee can hold two kinds of sessions. One involves meeting with a sample of business units to review the approach and to get their feedback. (Note: As a courtesy, the organizational steering committee should inform supervisors, middle managers, and union officials of the nature and content of the meetings before they are held.) The second kind of meeting is with a group of supervisors to determine their reaction to the strategy as well as to hear their business units' reactions to the information/feedback sessions (assuming that teams may not tell you everything they are thinking, especially if it is negative). An outline for a presentation to business units is included in Figure 4-6.

The biggest problem the committee will have with first-line supervisors is an unwillingness to reveal what they are really thinking if they believe it runs against the mainstream of the organization's leadership. They have developed their survival skills over the years, and one entrenched principle is "If you can't say something good, don't say anything at all." In this situation, an outside resource person, such as a consultant, who has been

A. Purpose of the Meeting

    1. Inform

    2. Clarify

    3. Get feedback

B. Explanation of the Team-based Strategy

    1. The structure

    2. The options considered for team strategies

    3. The steering committee's choice

    4. Rationale for the choice

C. Reactions to the Strategy

    1. Do you understand it?

    2. Will it work?

        If not, what alternative would you recommend?

        If so, are there any adjustments you would make?

D. Presentation of the Implementation Plan and Schedule

Figure 4-6. Outline for a Team Strategy Preview Meeting

working with the organization might be better able to gather the data than internal leadership.

The general idea is to test the waters. The steering committee should be prepared, however, for the extremes from no reaction to a ton of reasons why the approach will not work. It is up to the committee to sort out the concerns that need attention from the "noise" created by a system that is accustomed to one program after another that does not work. At the same time, the committee should be prepared for dissent hidden by silence or feigned agreement. The middle and first-line managers in most organizations have learned that it is easier to go along with something and then kill it when it hits the floor than to argue with the powers that be who have created and promoted the program. Work team members have seen this phenomenon again and again. Part of the "art" of change is to be sensitive to such factors and to find creative, effective ways to deal with them.

Leadership Team Development

The success of any long-term change effort depends on top management's ability to encourage and support the team concept. The leadership development process has to start with the top-level team. This effort complements and reinforces the involvement strategy at the first level of the organization.

If the organization is to change in any significant and permanent way, the existing or emerging leadership teams must also change. Experience has borne out the hypothesis that management teams need as much work as the rest of the organization. We generally find that first-level teams, be they task forces, problem-solving groups, business teams, or even self-managing teams, are far easier to launch and function at least as well as, if not better than, most management teams. And, if they are not working it shows immediately because they have less talent and desire to hide dysfunction. The failure of first-level teams is linked directly to the failure of management teams to shift the way they function in a long-term change effort. The leadership team development process permits the problems of the management teams to surface so that the managers at least have a chance of working with them. And, dealing with these problems provides the opportunity for the management team to develop new skills and behaviors. The leadership team development components are outlined in Figure 4-7.

The leadership development process has to start with the top-level team. Whatever one finds in the rest of the organization (good or bad) has its roots in the top leadership. So change managers must ignore the resistance in top

---

I. **Baseline Data**: A description of the team as it currently operates based on perceptions of others, team members' data, and observation

    A. Diagnostic process

    B. Questionnaire

    C. Observation

    D. Experiential (outdoor)

II. **Assessment of Strengths and Weaknesses**: Specification of the team's internal strengths (to build on) and weaknesses (to work on)

    A. Questionnaire

    B. Observation

    C. Experiential

III. **Alignment with New Vision**: Development of statements and documents that guide team development and functioning and that link leadership development to the overall organization's direction

    A. New role of the manager

    B. Leadership team mission

    C. Strategic plan

IV. **Leadership Development Curriculum**: The content and process of the development of the leadership team

    A. Leadership of a team environment

    B. Special interest topics

    C. New knowledge and skills

V. **Periodic Assessment and Adjustment**: The plan for monitoring and evaluating the team's plan and progress

---

Figure 4-7. Components of Leadership Team Development

management teams ("We don't have time"; "Middle management needs it more"; "We're already a team") and start at the top.

Part of the rationale for starting at the top is to have each level of management take responsibility for promoting and supporting (preferably even doing!) development with their team. This rationale serves two purposes. First, the managers in team development processes are not just "sponges" soaking up the team development experience. They are also in a train-the-trainer situation because they are going to lead the development effort for their respective teams. Second, initiating the team development process with the top leadership sends a powerful message to the entire organization about the future context. Although the process will take some time and effort, it is essential to effecting significant and permanent change in the organization.

Communication and Information Systems[*]

Communication and information systems are among the least understood, and most often ignored, elements of the transformation process. Information is a key control and influence tool in the new system. Yet, much of an organization's business information is not in a useful or understandable form and/or lacks credibility. In a change process, organizational communication shifts from its traditional role as a tool of management power to a new role as driver of change in the entire enterprise, where business information is developed for the level at which it is used.

---

[*]We are indebted to Lilot M. Moorman for her work in and counsel on issues related to communication and change.

Among the least understood and most often ignored elements of the organizational change process are the roles of communication and information systems. Most organizational leaders, management and union alike, confuse transmitting data with communication. Although information is the core of communication, simply giving information to someone does not mean you have communicated or that you have communicated what you intended. Many organizations spread information throughout the workplace (bulletin boards, meetings, newsletters, data printouts, etc.) yet still do not communicate well.

Business information is a key control and influence tool in the system. Management information, such as production and scrap printouts, the monthly financial summary, and the annual report, is essential to running the business. The problem with much management information is twofold. First, few people below the second-tier managers understand the information top managers use in making decisions. Second, if an effort is made to "move the data down," it is quickly found that the information is not in a useful form for first- and second-level teams. For example, reports may be cumulative for a department, while the production units are separate; or reports may be weekly or monthly (and often delayed), while the product is built daily or the service is ongoing. To be effective, business information must be organized along lines of production or service and must be available in a form understandable by the work force and in a timely manner.

Business information is also a key to attitude formation. What people read and hear, as well as what they do not read and hear, influences their attitudes. The credibility of the communicator and information is critical to effective communication. Many organizations give little thought to the effect of information and information systems on the attitudes, beliefs, and morale of employees. In a change process, communication plays out the drama of the new culture—taking risks, discussing "undiscussables," and demonstrating that the change is indeed happening. Appropriate communication can change the way people think about their work, their organization, and their roles.

The current state of communication and information systems in an organization both reflects the organization's systemic problem and contributes to the nature and persistence of that problem. Because the model is based on the principle that "everything is connected to everything else," communication will need to change along with other elements of the organization.

The change strategy positions communication and information systems in a unique role in which they reflect what is occurring in the new culture while at the same time driving the organization in the desired direction. Figure 4-8 lists some useful principles of effective organizational communication and outlines some roles of communication in the change process.

Assessing Organizational Communication and Developing A Strategy

Organizational communication and information systems can be assessed in two ways. One is through extracting information from the formal diagnostic process administered by the organizational steering committee. The second is through a separate survey of communication and information systems.

If the diagnostic process included a survey that had questions related to communication and information systems, the results can be isolated to create a specific picture of communication issues. Having interview data in addition to surveys allows the external consultant, in

Principles of Effective Communication and Information Systems

- Information must be communicated in a form that is understood.
- Systems must be in place to collect, organize, and transmit data.
- The information must be useful and presented in a timely way.
- Employees must be informed.
- Communication systems must deliver accurate information to the entire organization.
- Information must be credible and responsive to employee needs.
- Multiple avenues for communicating information should be used depending on the goal and type of information involved.

Goals and Functions of Communication in the Change Process

Education   Employees learn about the business and understand how the change process is driving new behaviors and outcomes.

Reflection   Employees see the shift to openness and trust reflected in the communication they receive. *What* issues are discussed and *how* they are discussed demonstrate that a different type of workplace is being created.

Support   Communication can support the change messages and actions. It is important that employees learn about successes as well as setbacks in the process.

Sense Making   Change communication meets employees' needs to predict, understand, and control the world around them as much as possible as well as their need to be recognized as individuals. It does so by giving people credible information in a timely way, by interpreting the news so people know what it means to them as individuals, and by recognizing individuals' contributions to the organization.

Attitude Formation   Communication has the ability to change the way people think about their work, their organization, and their roles. Well-planned, responsive communication focused on a few key messages can change people's perceptions about their work lives, their organization, and their fellow employees.

Figure 4-8. Elements of Communication and Information Systems

conjunction with a communication or steering committee, to construct a relatively accurate picture of the communication situation and needs. If such diagnostic data were not obtained, or if the diagnostic data are incomplete or insufficient, the steering committee or a communication committee can carry out its own communication assessment.

The alternative approach is to survey or interview business teams regarding what business information they need. This approach is critical if one is focusing on business information and information systems. It can also be used to assess organizational communication systems by using the same questions posed in a survey of the entire organization. We recommend collecting data as part of a team meeting.

The survey (and, if appropriate, interview) results are analyzed, and this information is then used to plan the development a communication strategy. Figure 4-9 includes a matrix for analyzing current communication tools and efforts, and Figure 4-10 lists issues to consider in designing the strategy. The details for developing a communication plan are provided in Chapter 5.

Assessing and Developing Business Information Systems

Most organizations' information systems were designed and are used for control from the top. In and of itself, this is not bad. The problem is, the information never gets to where the work is done, and if it did, it would not be in a form usable by work teams (or often even by midlevel business teams).

An information plan can be created with the same approach used for creating the communication system plan. The information plan is based on the goals and objectives of the business and on a survey of business/work

1. Fill out the table below by listing current communication system components in the left-hand column. Then analyze the extent to which each component contributes (positively or negatively) to the various goals of organizational communication based on data, perceptions, and other information. Use the following scale:

-5 -4 -3 -2 -1 0 1 2 3 4 5

Major   No   Major
Negative   Contribution   Positive
Contribution   Contribution

Current Communi-cation System Components	Goals and Functions of Organizational Communication				
	Educate	Reflect	Support	Sense Making	Attitude Formation
1.					
2.					
3.					
4.					

2. Once you have completed the analysis, answer the following questions.

- What is working in our current system?
- What is not working in our current system?
- Where do we fall short in communication?
- What techniques can we implement to fill the gaps?

Figure 4-9. Assessing Organizational Communication

Goals to Accomplish

- Open up the organization.
- Develop a new climate.
- Build a labor-management or management-employee partnership.
- Recognize the talent and skill of employees.
- Increase the credibility of leadership.

Themes/Messages to Emphasize

- People are the most important part of our organization.
- Quality is our most important product/service goal.
- We will take risks to get better and will live with the consequences.
- The organization's leadership will genuinely listen to employees' concerns.

The Best Way to Achieve Those Goals Is to Communicate

- *Business information*
  - the customer(s) and customer satisfaction
  - competition
  - schedule
  - cost
  - quality
  - capital spending
  - new business
- *Human interest information*
  - the people behind the work
  - the families of the people behind the work
- *Organizational information*
  - personnel changes
  - visitors
  - upcoming events
  - policy changes
  - community involvement

Means (Vehicles) for Communicating

- Electronic media: computer networks, electronic message boards
- Print media: newsletters, memoranda, special bulletins
- Face-to-face: departmental meetings, organizational meetings

Monitoring, Evaluating, and Improving Communication

- Use evaluation instruments.
- Meet with teams to discuss their reactions to the communication process.
- Check readership (how many newsletters are taken), attendance at meetings.

Figure 4-10. Issues in Designing a Communication Strategy

teams' information needs. Comparing the results of the survey with the goals of the organization will provide a planning base for business information systems.

To assess the information gaps in an organization, you can use the following process.

- Identify what information the teams are currently receiving.
- Identify what information the teams really need (and in what form).
- Determine where the teams will get the needed information.

The easiest way to obtain this information is probably through a business team survey. (A sample survey is provided in Figure 4-11). This survey can be completed by individual members of a team or by the whole team (on the basis of consensus). The results will point the organization in the right direction concerning what information needs to be where and on what schedule.

The following principles should be applied in developing information systems.

- Every business unit and team should receive regular (at least once a week), timely (within a day or two), usable feedback on their critical performance indicators.
- Business information should be in a form understandable by the business unit and should contain information related to the unit's business and performance.
- Different systems should provide business information for various levels of the organization; that is, there should be one system (or vehicle) that reports overall business (e.g., the factory or

To conduct this survey:

1. Have a sample of business team leaders or members identify the key "Team Success Indicators. "

2. Collect data from the team by

   a. Having individual team members fill out the form, or
   b. Having the team as a whole complete the form on a consensus basis.

3. Analyze the results and use them to create a business information plan.

Team Success Indicators	What type of information is needed to track the indicator?	What is the source of the information?	How often do you need to receive it?	Who is currently responsible for obtaining it?
Schedule				
Budget				
Quality				
Customer Satisfaction				
Other				
Other				
Other				

Figure 4-11. Sample Business Team Information Needs Survey

division) performance, one that reports the business group (e.g., the department's), performance, and one that reports the specific business unit (e.g., the team's) performance.

The first step in the plan is creation of the "big picture." The survey data and other information will provide the basis for determining the overall needs in the organization. The survey data can be supplemented by anecdotal data.

The overall communication strategy should account for selection and transmission of organizational information. The business unit manager and steering committee are responsible for identifying and communicating critical department data. The hub of a business unit's information system is the unit's key performance indicators. These indicators (quality, cost, productivity, scrap, etc.) create two requirements: (1) they tell the business unit what to pay attention to, and (2) they serve as the benchmark against which to make future comparisons.

Organizational Issues and Constituencies

The final component of the change strategy addresses any major or unresolved issues in the organization at large or issues/needs among constituencies within the organization. These issues usually become apparent in the diagnostic process, but they may also surface as the organization moves through the change effort. Task forces are used to address these issues.

The final component of the change strategy is addressing the major unresolved issues—business and people—in the organization. Examples of unresolved issues are an out-of-date corporate policy, a long-standing practice that is in the way of improvements, motivation systems and structures, or a quality-of-work-life issue. Resolving such issues will occupy major time and energy among departments and employees. A constituency, such as supervisors or union leadership, may also have issues needing resolution.

The important issues and constituencies will typically surface during the diagnostic process. This occurs not so much because great discoveries are made through the diagnosis but because the diagnosis is the organization's first major attempt at listening. In so doing, many of the "open secrets" (something that almost everyone knows but few will discuss openly) come to light.

The organizational steering committee will never find itself short of things to work on, but will find it difficult to isolate the most critical issues to pursue. Task forces can be used to address these issues, but the organization of these groups requires special attention. To determine what issues a task force should pursue, the steering committee should ask the following questions.

- Does this issue affect a significant segment of the organization?
- Will resolving the issue remove a major barrier or help us move in the direction of the vision?
- Would resolution of this issue send a message to the organization about the value and legitimacy of this process (does it have symbolic value)?

If the answer is "yes" to one or more of these questions, the organizational steering committee should think about how to address the issue.

A task force requires planning and development. These requirements are outlined in the last section of this chapter. To ensure the success of a task force once members have been oriented and trained, the following aspects should be considered.

- *Supporting the task force.* If there is staff for the change process (see Chapter 6), they should be assigned to support the task force. Support can take the form of facilitating meetings or, at a minimum, of sitting in on meetings and providing help when needed.

- *Making the task force accountable.* Often task forces are not held accountable for the outcomes of their work. By being clear about their charge, specifying the desired outcomes, and requiring that the task force evaluate the outcomes, the steering committee solidifies the accountability of the group.

- *Recognizing good work.* If a task force does a good job, the organization should recognize them. Too often, we assume that good work is the norm (and, therefore, nothing need be done) and that poor work should be criticized or punished. Neither is the case. If the group does poorly, the steering committee should see what they might need to improve their efforts (training, resources, assistance). If the group does well, the steering committee should find a way to say thanks (e.g., a lunch, a token of appreciation such as a certificate, public recognition such as an article in the company newsletter).

Many organizations simply name a group of people to serve on a task force, give them a general charge and a deadline, and send them off to do their work. The results often reflect the quality of the effort in putting the group together. Before a group is named, a focused discussion should be held on the following questions.

- Who should participate in the task force? Who are the major stakeholders involved? Who has critical data or expertise needed to do the work in the task force? Who should be permanent members of the task force as opposed to resources to the task force on an as-needed basis?

- What are the goals of the task force? What should be the outcome if they are successful in doing their job?
- What is the time frame for the task force's work (deadline)? Are there interim checkpoints at which they should deliver products or reports?
- Do the members need some special training or preparation (task or relationship) in order to be effective?

Given the objectives, the task, and the composition of the task force, decide what data or information the members may need to get their work done well, and develop a plan to give them access to it. Make available or accessible any technical or educational resources they may need. Make sure the consequences of good performance are favorable. Also consider the kind of ongoing leadership and managerial support that will be provided and whether training should be provided for the members. Finally, develop a plan and process to track and support the work of the task force. Then use the data to help them improve.

5

IMPLEMENTING THE CHANGE PROCESS

Orientations: Introducing the Organization to the Change Process

The first step in implementing the change process is to inform the work force about it. This communication is best done through orientation sessions sponsored by the organizational steering committee. These sessions provide the opportunity to inform the organization about the process and allow leaders to voice their commitment; the sessions also set the tone for the future.

An orientation process has a minimum of three important purposes.

1. Fundamentally, it is a communication effort. The steering committee *informs* the entire organization about the process—what it is, why it is being done, what people can expect to happen, and what their roles are in the process.

2. It is an opportunity for the organization's leaders to plant a symbolic stake representing their commitment to change through a team-based strategy. By "going public," they will find it difficult to abandon the effort.

3. It is a time to set a tone for the future. The orientation is not just a collection of boring presentations. It is an occasion of excitement and challenge for the future. At the same time, it should be realistic. It will not be easy to tell everyone there will be more failures than successes in the short run, and it will be hard for many to change. But saying so up front sends a message about the new kind of effort being put into place.

The guiding principles for the orientation process are as follows:

- The orientation should be conducted face-to-face. A written document should not be the only tool used to announce and explain the effort. (A letter from the leadership might be a way to announce the process and to invite employees to attend an orientation when it is held, but it is not a substitute for the real thing.) Video is not a good option either, unless this is a very large organization. If a video is necessary, it should be shown in conjunction with in-person, "local" leadership.

- The content and tone of the presentation should be honest and straightforward. It is important for employees to hear straight talk, not a commercial for a new "program."

- The orientation should spell out realistic expectations. It is better to be on the conservative side about what to expect than to overstate what one will do. Then everyone can celebrate exceeding the expectations rather than being disappointed.

- Leaders of the transformation process should conduct as many orientations as needed to involve everyone in the organization.

A sample outline for an orientation program is presented in Figure 5-1.

Orientations can be done either before or after the diagnostic process. If done before, the orientation sessions might be a place to administer a survey or to invite volunteers for interviews. If held after the diagnosis, orientations can refer to the results of the diagnostic

Topic	Presenter	Time (Minutes)
Welcome and Introductions	Top leader/Union leader	2–5
Introduce the organizational steering committee, internal support staff, and consultants (if you use them).		
Overview of the Change Effort	Internal or External Consultant	30
Have the "expert" present an overview of organizational change.		
The Plan for Your Organization	Steering committee	10–15
Have the steering committee outline the goals of the effort and the activities that will occur in the next six to twelve months.		
Diagnostic Activity or Feedback	Steering committee	10–15
Have the steering committee present a "straight talk" summary of the diagnosis.		
Commitment to the Effort	Steering committee	5
Have the steering committee offer a formal statement of commitment from top executive(s) and union leadership.		
What's Next?	Steering committee	2–3
Have the steering committee provide a more detailed description of the next couple of steps in the process.		

Figure 5-1. Orientation Program Outline

process in a discussion of what changes the organization needs to make. Either way will work; it is primarily a matter of what feels right to those involved.

Awareness Sessions: Preparing the Organization for Change

The primary goals in preparing the organization for change are to give employees an understanding of the

> team-based process and to help them see the "picture"
> resulting from the diagnosis. Awareness sessions are
> used to bring a cross section of the organization to-
> gether for two days. These are not training sessions,
> but an opportunity to understand the organization in
> new ways. These sessions actually set the stage for
> the change process.

The preparation process gives employees a sense of what the organizational change process is all about and affirms that it is not "just another program. " Participants should be encouraged to talk about the organization's pathology as they experience it and to see the interconnectedness of everything in the organization.

Awareness sessions can be used to provide an opportunity for employees to understand the organization in new ways, to see other constituents differently, and to size up the process. In addition, the process of "healing" can begin as diverse groups begin to share their data and to experience the "pain" of the organization from each other's perspective. Sessions can also be used to help the organizational members start to understand the relationship between the organization's pathologies and the content of the change strategy.

Preparing the organization is not a training process; it is part of laying the groundwork for change. In training, organizations expect and want some change in participants' attitudes or behavior. Here, however, the goal is for leadership to experience the effects of existing structures, processes, and belief systems and to talk about the future they would like to create.

Awareness sessions can be configured in different ways, depending on the approach chosen by the organization steering committee. The goal is to get a variety of people in the room together for a two-day period. We have found that about thirty to thrity-five people is the maximum for a good session and that twenty is a bare minimum. Participants in a given session should include a vertical (levels of management) and horizontal (managers from different functional areas) mix of participants. If the business has organized labor, union officials should be included in the sessions. If there are no unions, staff and hourly employees (five to eight per session) should be included.

Planning effective awareness sessions takes into account topics (what subjects should be covered?); activities (how should sessions be conducted?); and the presenter/ facilitator (who conducts the session?). The topics are based on the key areas of change in the human system: leadership and decision making, competition and cooperation among functional areas, communication and listening, motivation, effective teams (problem solving), organizational change, and if unionized, labor-management relations. Sessions have the greatest impact when they involve a minimum of presentation. Instead they should focus on exercises that generate data about the nature of the current organization and what people want for the future, with sufficient discussion time allowed for various views and emotions to be aired. Figure 5-2 offers a sample agenda for an awareness session.

The steering committee should allow time at some point to relate the results of the diagnosis to the session topics and to relate the various topics to each other and to the organization. It is usually not possible to cover all the possible subjects in a two-day period. Therefore, the steering committee needs to decide which areas are most critical in understanding the organization and in getting people ready to experience and support the change process.

The most effective sessions, at least at the outset of a process, are conducted by outside people. This is not

Goals of the Awareness Session

- Orient organizational leadership to the concept of organizational transformation and to the change model being used.
- Build on the diagnostic "picture" of the organization as the basis for determining where the organization is at present.
- Explore the organization of the future as the basis of the design for change.
- Begin to describe the structure, roles, and strategies of the elements of the change process.
- Model the change process—its values and behaviors—for the organization of the future.
- Build overall understanding of and commitment to the organizational change effort.

Presentation of Topics

For each topic, include

1. An overview of the topic and its relationship to organization performance.

2. An exercise on the topic out of which emerge data on both the organization at present and how participants would like it to be.

3. Discussion about the nature of the data from the exercise and how it translates in your organization.

As you move through the topics, the pattern of your organization will begin to emerge, and the exercises and discussions will begin to have a "connectedness" to them.

Daily Agenda

Day 1

- Introduction and overview of the awareness session
- Description of the current organization: summary of the diagnosis
- Leadership and decision making

Figure 5-2. Awareness Session Agenda

- Motivation
- Cooperation and competition
- Customer satisfaction
- Summary of the day

Day 2
- Resolving conflict
- Problem solving
- Leadership and change
- The change strategy
- Conclusion and evaluation

Figure 5-2. Awareness Session Agenda (continued)

necessarily because they have more expertise, but because they are outsiders. Without an investment in the current organization, the outsider can hear things differently and can speak more openly.

If you have internal staff in place to support the change process, the external consultant/presenter should have the responsibility of developing this staff. The preparation sessions are a wonderful opportunity for internal staff to introduce themselves to the organization, understand the organization in a new way, and to practice their skills.

Implementing the Participation Strategy: Launching and Supporting Teams

Creating teams must be done in the context of the larger organization change effort. Training should provide team members with better interpersonal skills, a working understanding of team dynamics, and an overview of the basics of business operations.

The key to creating successful teams lies in establishing clear goals for them, carefully preparing them, and supporting them once they are in operation. Implementing the teams should not be viewed as merely a structural issue (who is in what team for what purpose) or a training issue (what skills teams need to do their job). Either approach would diminish the teams' long-term contributions and chances of survival.

As Figure 5-3 demonstrates, team development should encompass three elements: (1) interpersonal and team dynamic skills—how people relate to each other and how teams pull together to get work accomplished; (2) productivity improvement—how teams can identify, map, and improve their processes; and (3) the basics of business

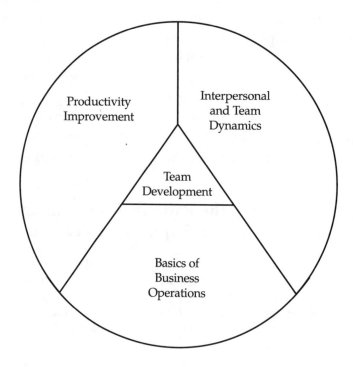

Figure 5-3. Elements of Team Development

operations—how the unit fits into the larger business. Launching effective teams requires varying degrees of all three kinds of development. A common tendency is to focus exclusively on business or problem-solving skills. But, for example, if the organization is implementing teams and the members of the team do not trust each other or their supervisor, the result is likely to be a dysfunctional group. Or, if a team is already cohesive but has no sense of the business, the team effort may or may not improve anything.

Launching and developing teams is different than just training them. Team development is more than skill development. It also involves both enculturation and deculturation. On the one hand, you are putting a team into place and beginning to create a special culture in that team (enculturation). On the other hand, you are beginning to separate (alienate) the team from many elements of the existing culture so that they begin to "seed" the organization of the future (deculturation).

The process of developing the team can be compared to learning to play golf (a complex behavior). One can take lessons, but actually playing well is a product of lots of practice, continuing coaching, and additional training where necessary.

Providing support to teams involves monitoring and coaching. The coaches (internal consultants, external consultants, or steering committee members) sit in on meetings and problem-solving sessions, give feedback to team leaders, coach and counsel, and oversee team self-evaluations.

Team Training

Training is an ongoing process and a function of the team-based strategy. The curriculum varies depending on team type, while the pace varies depending on the availability of teams to pursue training. The training can be done by an external consultant, but using internal staff at some point has a greater advantage in the long run.

Training is an ongoing process and a function of the team-based strategy. Although it is developed by the organizational steering committee, training needs reinforcement by managers and supervisors to be successful. Some teams will learn faster than others. If the change effort focuses resources on those teams that excel, the other teams will be pulled along.

The training curriculum varies depending on the nature of the team, as shown in Table 5-1. Task forces and problem-solving teams require highly focused training, while business team training is much more extensive. Training can be done internally or externally. The steering committee may want to call on outside consultants or someone they recommend. However, since one of the goals in the process is to achieve independence from outside assistance, the organization steering committee should address the strategy for achieving independence in team development. There are two options: The organization's training and development specialists can work with the consultants in delivering the training modules so they can learn the content and process of delivery, or the organization can create a pool of part-time, temporary trainers from within the salaried and hourly staff (you will be amazed at how much talent is buried in your departments).

Development of this internal staff is a four-step process: (1) train the trainers (in training skills and content

*Table 5-1. Training Module Recommendations
for Various Team Types*

Curriculum Module	Type of Team			
	Task Force	Problem-Solving Team	Business Team	Self-directed Team
Interpersonal and Team Dynamics				
Orientation to change			X	X
Mission and purpose of the team	X	X	X	X
Vision and the ideal team				X
Team business meetings			X	X
Decision making in the team			X	X
Problem solving in the team	X	X	X	X
Learning styles in the team				X
Roles in the team				X
Contracting for the future				X
Evaluation of the team and improvement		X	X	X
Communication, listening, and feedback	X	X	X	X
Conflict strategies and interest negotiation	X	X	X	X
Productivity Improvement				
Process analysis			X	X
Productivity improvement overview			X	X
Supplier analysis for the business				X
Customer analysis for the business				X
Quality and continuous improvement			X	X
Business information for the team			X	X
Basics of Business Operations				
Overview of the business			X	X
Team profile: What business are you in?			X	X
Roles in the organization				X
Business planning: Part I				X
Business planning: Part II				X

mastery), (2) have them observe delivery of the module, (3) supervise their delivery of the module, and (4) have them deliver the module on their own.

Creating an internal pool of trainers has several advantages. With fewer promotions, many employees will find the opportunity to contribute and grow as a training resource and the subsequent recognition to be tremendous motivators. A permanent cadre of trainers (and after they are experienced, coaches) is a wonderful resource in the organization. Furthermore, the trainers are in the middle of the workplace where the teams function day-to-day, so they are available when people need them.

The pace of the training is a function of both team type and operational availability. Task forces or problem-solving groups require relatively compact training experiences that extend, at most, for two or three weeks (if training is broken into "bite-sized" packages). Business teams and self-managing work groups require a series of development experiences designed to increase skills and to build a team. If the pace is too fast, the team members fail to incorporate the learning into their work, and the value simply dissipates. If the pace is too slow, team members may lose interest or come to believe that the effort is not serious. Moreover, the pace of training should take into consideration and complement other operational imperatives. If relatively few demands are made on any given team, training may progress rapidly. If, however, the business is pushed to its limits and time away from operational responsibilities is an issue, the training schedule will be more diffused. Either way, the organizational steering committee or a representative task force should consider and decide on implementation speed and duration.

Team Leader/Facilitator Training

All teams need someone to organize, guide, and co-ordinate their work. This someone is the task force chair, team leader, or group facilitator. For such leaders to be up to the role, they need training specific to their needs.

Regardless of the kind of team used, someone needs to organize, guide, and coordinate its work: a task force chair, team leader, or group facilitator. It is in the long-term best interest of the organization to develop strong facilitation skills in management, supervision, and, if applicable, union leadership. Doing so permeates the organization not only with talent but also with an orientation to leadership that is quite different from the traditional command-demand style.

Creating effective facilitators is difficult. Current managers and supervisors have been recruited, trained, and rewarded by the old system. Many are not naturally suited for facilitation. Surprisingly, a number of first-line supervisors do not like being in front of a group or running a team meeting. As a result, they will often be uncomfortable with the new team process.

One alternative to using existing managers is to create a pool of facilitators who are available to teams and departments. This group would consist of hourly and salaried employees who are interested in something beyond their job and who are trained in facilitation methodology and skills. (If the organization is unionized, union representatives and bargaining unit members should also be involved.) These facilitators function much like the pool of trainers discussed in "Team Training" earlier in this chapter. In general, we do not recommend this approach. Although it fills a need and reduces the anxiety of existing managers and supervisors, it props up the existing system, reducing a valuable learning opportunity and removing the tension for change. An option is to create a resource pool using existing managers and supervisors.

Figure 5-4 outlines a recommended curriculum for training facilitators. Sufficient coaching and group practice should be built into the training. In addition, facilitators may pair up in a "buddy system" to observe and coach each other when they begin their work. This seems to be a low-threat, high-payoff approach to development.

Developing the Leadership Team

Development of the leadership team is difficult because this team must lead the change process while simultaneously learning to work as a team. The top-down team development should be done along with a bottom-up participation effort. The process begins by opening up the management and defining its culture. In conjunction with a consultant, the team develops the curriculum in a two-day session.

Developing the leadership team is a difficult process because this team must lead the change effort within the organization while simultaneously learning to work as a team. It is important to take a long-term approach to leadership team development, as quick fixes and one-shot efforts fade easily.

The development process includes defining the organizational/management team culture—what it is and what it should be; creating the leadership team development curriculum; implementing the leadership team development curriculum; assessing growth; and contracting for the future.

The first leadership development event is critical. It will set the tone for the team and lay the groundwork for succeeding sessions. The team needs to commit at least two

I. Task and Process in Groups
   A. What it is
   B. How it works

II. Role of the Facilitator
   A. In task (problem-solving team meetings)
   B. In process

III. Handling of Difficult People

IV. Use of Flip Charts

V. Effective and Ineffective Groups
   A. Characteristics of each
   B. Role of the facilitator

VI. Logistics of Team Events
   A. Scheduling
   B. Room setup
   C. Minutes/records
   D. Proposals and presentations
   E. Use of resource people

VII. Experiential Learning (video)
   A. Task or problem
   B. Review
   C. Coaching

VIII. Monitoring and Evaluation of Teams and Facilitation
   A. Use of surveys
   B. Group assessments
   C. Getting and giving feedback

Figure 5-4. Training Curriculum for Leaders and Facilitators

consecutive days to the initial event. Consecutive days are necessary because a major shift often occurs in the team from the first to the second day. This shift tends not to occur if the two days are separated.

Two common approaches are used. One is to construct a two-day classroom event with lectures, exercises, simulations, and discussions. The other, increasingly popular in the last five years, is the outdoor team-building experience combined with a classroom component. Figure 5-5 is a typical agenda for a two-day event with an outdoor team-building component.

The process of team development starts with understanding where the team is and defining where the team wants to be. The development process itself is then designed to help the team move in the direction of the organization's vision. This approach to team development allows one to customize the activities for the team. Although a number of useful team development training programs are available, using them without conducting the team-specific analysis risks either doing some unnecessary work or missing some key issues.

We recommend that the team take responsibility, with the aid and assistance of an expert in the change process, for defining its developmental needs. Once team members have assessed their cultural roots and team dynamics, they will be ready to create a management development curriculum that addresses their weaknesses and develops new, dynamic behaviors for managing in a team-based organization.

Leadership team development sessions can be held every two weeks or at least once a month. The sessions can last from three hours to six hours, depending on the nature of the topic, team energy, and outside commitments. Not every topic of team development or every

Evening Before

Introductory Session
- Overview of the change process
- Purpose and nature of management team development
- Overview of the two-day process

(Note: You can also administer a culture or group styles assessment instrument at this time to provide time to score it and prepare the results.)

Day One

Outdoor Team Building Exercises—Daytime
- Introduction and warm up
- Orientation to the day
- Team building exercises

Evening Session
- One or two indoor team-building exercises (optional)
- Discussion of
  - Lessons learned
  - Implications for the team
  - Strengths and weaknesses of the team and its process

Day Two

Review of the Team Culture or Group Styles Assessment
- Results
- Implications for the team: behavior change

A Picture of the Team
- Combining Day One data with the team culture/group styles survey results

A Vision for the Team

What the Team Needs to Get to the Vision

Team Charter
- Creation and commitment to long-term team development curriculum

Figure 5-5. Sample Introductory Curriculum
for Leadership Team Development

team development session need be facilitated by the same consultant. It is a good idea to bring in different experts where appropriate. Each module must have exercises that both translate the concepts into practice and give the team a way to apply the learning to their day-to-day practice.

Implementing the Communication System

A communications plan provides guidance for the various communication vehicles. It should be based on the vision of the organization and the goals of the transformation process. This plan is often created by a communication committee or a subcommittee of the organizational steering committee.

Many organizations implement communication activities without a plan. Some enthusiastic employee or committee will devote a lot of time and energy to creating a newsletter, for example, but be off the mark in content or tone. Without guidance and vision as well as a view of how various communication vehicles affect their audience, the organization loses a major opportunity.

The communication plan is often created by a communication committee, formed by and accountable to the organizational steering committee. An alternative is to have a subcommittee of the organizational steering committee create the plan. Figure 5-6 shows a sample outline of a communication plan.

The plan should be based on the vision of the organization and the goals of the change process in the area of communication. After goals, perhaps the most important element of the plan is the messages or *themes* of communication. These themes are the basis for designing the content and tone of all vehicles; they are the descriptions that the committee would like to have members make of the organi-

Goals

1. Employees will understand the business.
2. Employees will perceive the site as a good place to work.
3. Employees will have improved attitudes and morale.
4. The work site will make significant progress toward becoming a performance leader.
5. The change process will be aided.

Success Criteria

The communication processes should meet the following criteria:

- Accuracy
- Honesty
- Openness
- Timeliness
- Credibility
- Consistency
- Responsiveness to employees' information wants and needs
- Proactivity (deal with issues before-the-fact)

Themes or Messages to Communicate

1. The business is becoming a profitable performance leader characterized by

   - A quality-driven process.
   - A customer focus (internally and externally).
   - Safety consciousness.
   - A diversity orientation.

2. The majority of employees like working in and are proud to be a part of the business.
3. The employees are beginning to work together as a team (rather than as individuals) to produce a high-quality product/service.
4. Management listens, responds, and is open to new ideas.
5. Management cares about the people who work here.

Figure 5-6. Sample Outline of a Communication Plan

Communication Vehicles

At a minimum, the following communication vehicles should be considered for inclusion in the strategy:

1. Departmental meetings (weekly or biweekly)
2. Business review meetings (semiannually)
3. Telephone call-in information system
4. Electronic message boards
5. Newsletter (weekly or biweekly)

Figure 5-6. Sample Outline of a Communication Plan (continued)

zation some time in the future. For example, one communication committee chose as a theme: "We want the organization to care as much about its people as it does about its product."

From themes, the committee moves to logistical planning. The first step is to identify key vehicles in communication, such as meetings, newsletters, and electronic message boards. It is best to make no assumptions about what to do. Committees often limit themselves by assuming that they have to make use of what is in place. Instead, they should plan as if starting from scratch. If some workable tools are in place, all the better. The "meat" of the plan is the definition of the role, the characteristics, and the logistics (who, what, when, etc.) of each tool. Finally, the committee should prepare resources, including staff, budget, and schedule for the communication plan.

Implementing the Resolution of Organizational Issues

When dealing with organizational issues and groups' concerns, it is important to resist the temptation to treat the symptom as the problem. Such issues and concerns are really products of the larger system problems, and as such they must be seen as part of the overall strategy.

Handling the "resolution of organizational issues" segment of the change model requires a special sensitivity. On one hand, the kinds of issues identified and the groups addressed are critical factors in the operation of the organization. On the other, the temptation is to treat the symptom as the problem, missing the fact that such issues and group concerns are really products of the larger system problems.

Treating the issues and concerns as symptoms means viewing them as part of the overall strategy. Resolving them helps build momentum for change, models how the organization should run in the future, and presumably generates data about how such approaches are better than the more traditional approach.

We once worked with a corporation that had contracted for a national survey of its employees. The survey results were compiled by plant, division, and corporate level. Next, analysis committees were organized, one for each level of data (corporate, division, plant). Their task was to identify problems at their respective organizational level, prioritize them, and organize a strategy for solving the problems. The committees held meetings, made proposals, formed task forces, and implemented solutions. Even though the items on the immediate lists were checked off and reported to corporate as "solved," two years later each level of the corporation could have generated a new, equally long and important list of unresolved issues. Why?

Because this approach dealt with the symptoms of the organization, not its real problems.

It is important to understand that this corporation's approach to solving symptoms and the approach to resolving issues and group concerns described in this model may appear similar on the surface, but they differ radically in their perspective on the task, in use of data from the effort, and in expectations for outcomes.

The following sections provide two summaries of special issues and constituencies projects from change efforts. One example is a task force that was used to give first-line supervisors a platform and the leverage to influence the definition of their future role and to create strategies to help ensure that they achieved that role. The second example addresses the gap between change efforts and the collective bargaining process. Here we describe the strategy called the "labor-management forum," in which the union and management come together to work on bargaining-related issues and their overall relationship using the strategies and techniques of the change process.

Changing the Role of Supervision

One key organizational issue requiring resolution is the role of supervisors. If the change strategy does not adequately address this group, the steering committee can establish a task force to develop guidelines, recommendations, and strategies to facilitate transformation of supervision from the traditional model to a model that supports the organization's vision.

Paramount to permanent change in the organization's culture is a change in the norms, procedures, and behaviors of critical groups within that culture, including supervisory groups. When we reviewed change processes that had been in place three or four years in the early 1980s, we found, almost without exception, that the change had not permeated the ranks of supervisors. At best, in most cases they were tolerating or going along with the effort.

On the surface, such tolerance seems sufficient (especially to top managers, who are not accustomed to knowing what is really going on in the workplace anyway). Everyone at and below the level of the supervisors knows, however, that the change is only temporary. The question is: How does the organization get permanent change in supervisors to bring their role and function in line with the vision? Surely, a foundation exists in the vision and goals that have been created for the process, which are supported by structures and activities that create environments and behaviors to model the organization of the future. Still, these are usually not enough.

The steering committee might consider expanding the strategy to address a specific constituency—first-line supervision. Sending a memorandum or holding a meeting to tell supervision what is expected of them will not do the job; nor will calling one or two of the "bad guys" into the office for a tongue-lashing. Instead, the strategy should be to use an overall approach. Figure 5-7 is a summary of the structure and implementation of a task force on the future of supervision in the organization. Such a task force can create a structure within which supervisors can begin to work. That structure should be designed (with and by the supervisors) so that the behaviors, activities, and outcomes are consistent with, and move the organization toward, the vision.

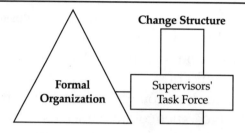

Purpose: To develop guidelines, recommendations, and strategies to facilitate the transformation of supervision from the traditional model to a model that will support the organization's vision.

Membership: Supervisors representing various constituencies.

Size: Six to ten people.

Duration: Six months to two years, depending on the scope of their work.

Areas of Interest

Role of Supervision in the Future. As the change process unfolds, new roles and relationships will evolve between supervisors and their work teams, other supervisors, their superiors, and staff areas. The task force develops a generic statement or document to describe the role of the supervisor in the new work environment.

Development of Supervision in the New Role. The future role and function of supervision should drive supervisor development processes. Based on the organization change model used and on the role statement developed by the task force, the task force designs and recommends a training and development program and process to help develop the supervisor of the future.

Performance Appraisal, Recognition, and Promotion. The performance appraisal, recognition, and promotion processes in the organization should reflect and encourage the new model of management and supervision. The task force reviews current practices in the organization (and elsewhere) as a foundation for designing and recommending policies and procedures for the future.

Note: A task force can focus on one or all of the above (including perhaps a process for selecting supervisors in the future). However, it is our belief that the role definition process is the key to the next two, so the task force should begin its work there.

Figure 5-7. Task Force on the Future of Supervision in the Organization

Bridging the Gap Between Organizational Change and Collective Bargaining

In a unionized workplace, collective bargaining efforts should be integrated with the change strategy to avoid conflicts that can stall or halt the process. Creating a labor-management forum bridges the gap between the traditional environment of collective bargaining and that of the new culture.

During the 1980s, in unionized workplaces a schism often developed between employee involvement efforts and collective bargaining. Because collective bargaining was the terrain on which the old battles had occurred and from which hostility and animosity had their roots, employee involvement processes purposely avoided issues and processes of that domain. Labor leaders and management constructed employee involvement efforts that dealt with non-negotiable items and that steered clear of such things as grievances. Furthermore, joint steering committees would often make plans for suspending a process during collective bargaining and for restarting the effort if bargaining involved a labor dispute.

Over time, however, a successful change effort will eventually bump up against the collective bargaining process. When this happens, neither the collective bargaining structure nor the joint change process has the license or the tools to address the issues. And, depending on the structure of the business and the bargaining unit, it may be impossible to get at the heart of some issues. (For example, some facility representation units are actually part of a larger collective bargaining unit, the leadership of which is not a part of the change process.)

Another problem emerges when the collective bargaining domain (labor relations and committee members) continue a traditional hostile, adversarial relationship amid attempts to create a new culture in the workplace. Such hostility can quickly and significantly affect any efforts to change the climate of labor-management relations.

Our recommendation in such cases is to address the gap between changing the culture and collective bargaining by (1) creating a structure containing key stakeholders, and (2) having the structure behave in ways that both model and reinforce the culture one is trying to create.

One way to accomplish this task is to create a labor-management forum. An outline for creating such a forum is provided in Figure 5-8. The strategy in the forum is to create a "safe house" to which the parties (labor, management, labor relations) can bring issues from the collective bargaining arena (or that will end up there if not resolved) and address them with norms and tools developed in the culture change process. This is a simple but powerful strategy to effect change in one key area of the organization.

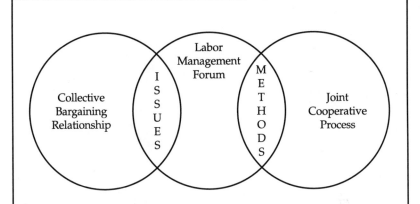

Purpose: To provide a "bridge" to link collective bargaining issues to the philosophy, values, skills, and methodolo-
gies of the transformation process.

Membership: Key labor relations staff, union committee members,
key managers.

Size: Ten to twelve members (if you have more, consider
setting up separate forums).

When: When the change process is sufficiently mature or
when collective bargaining issues begin to get in the
way of the change process.

How: Select members.

Hold a training session out of which come the
following:

- Vision for the forum
- Statement of principles of operating the forum
- Specification of critical success factors
- Consensus statement on the role of the forum
  (as opposed to other structures)
- Consensus statement on the role of participants
  (as opposed to other roles)
- Agreement on how to run the forum
- Logistics plan

Figure 5-8. Creating a Labor-Management Forum

6

MANAGING THE CHANGE PROCESS

Supporting and Administering the Change Process

An organizational change process cannot occur on its own and should not be administered solely within existing organizational structures. Internal staff and external consultants must be used to support and administer the change process.

Experience indicates that a major organizational change process does not occur on its own and in fact requires outside help. This situation is due primarily to the fact that existing organizational structures are part of the problem. In addition, few organizations have the perspective or the talent to support the change process.

Internal staff and external consultants perform two primary functions in the change process: administration/coordination and consulting. Administration/coordination tasks include scheduling activities, supporting events, coordinating various elements of the process, and communicating between committees and groups. Consulting tasks include providing facilitation, training, organizational communication, change management, and expert assistance to the effort. As time passes (and depending on the level of internal expertise), internal staff move from an emphasis on administration to a greater role in consulting. External consultants, conversely, spend the early stages of the process helping with structure and design; then change their emphasis to consulting in the middle stages as the process begins to work; and in the final stage move away from the organization while developing internal resources to fill the gap.

Our organizational behavior model is the basis for understanding the role of internal and external assistance in the change process. As illustrated in Figure 6-1, internal staff and external consultants focus on the intervention

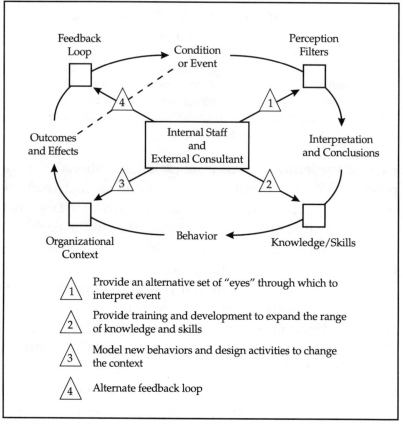

Figure 6-1. Role of Internal Staff and External Consultants

elements of the organizational behavior model. They provide the following:

- An objective set of lenses through which organizational events can be viewed, which often provides an alternative to the existing paradigms.

- Training and development to expand organizational members' knowledge and skills, thus offering a wider range of options when a response is needed.

- Modeling of appropriate organizational behavior for a new context by being open and honest, listening well, managing conflict productively, and so forth.

- Designing and carrying out organizational activities that (a) help change the organizational context and (b) create new or alternative feedback loops in the organization.

The staff and consultants may be performing a number of roles simultaneously in any given activity.

Phases of the Change Process

The organizational steering committee and the internal coordinator carry the primary responsibility for managing the transformation process. Typically, large-scale change efforts progress through five phases: planning and preparation, implementation, adaptation, renewal, and maturity.

Managing the change process is as important to the success of the process as managing a business is to the success of the business. The primary management role falls to the organizational steering committee and the internal coordinator. Although the external consultant initially plays a big part in the management process, this task is soon transferred to the internal coordinator(s) and the organizational steering committee to reduce the dependency on outside help.

Change management is tricky. One way to focus on appropriate change management activities is to understand that large-scale change progresses through five phases: planning and preparation, implementation, adaptation, renewal, and maturity. These phases are for the most part linear, but they often overlap without clear boundaries. Moreover, although the phases offer a great model for understanding the evolution of the change process, at some point large-scale change takes on a life of its own, and the phases may no longer be accurate. Nevertheless, the phase approach provides a good basis for appropriate change management activities.

Phase One is the planning and preparation phase. At this stage an organizational steering committee sketches out what they want to achieve in the change process, hire help, and plan the strategy and structure of the process. Next, the organization is introduced to the process through orientation and awareness sessions.

This first phase is characterized by excitement on the part of the few who organized and planned everything, and by skepticism and questioning on the part of the majority who are being introduced to the change for the very first time. Activities that occur during the planning and preparation phase include creation of the mission, vision, and value statements; a diagnostic process and feedback sessions; work force orientations; and awareness sessions. The change management emphasis in the initial planning and preparation stage includes getting plans made, involving as many people as possible, choosing a coordinator (or coordinators), completing the diagnostic and feedback process, and helping to start up, orient, and organize adjunct committees.

Phase Two is the implementation phase. Here the planning of Phase One is put into place. The participation team strategy, which involves team orientation and team training, should be started. The leadership development process should be put in place and started, which may mean monthly or biweekly leadership development sessions. The communication arm of the change process should begin. Thus, a communication design committee should be formed, oriented, and asked to design a communication strategy for the process. Finally, any task forces or adjunct committees to deal with special issues or constituencies should be started. These may include a supervisors' task force, a labor-management committee, or a rewards and recognition team.

This phase is characterized as activity based—the business-unit-level steering committees will be busy "forming"; trainers will be selected and training will be started; adjunct committees will be formed, members selected, plans made; the communication process will take some form; and people will be attending more and more meetings and team events.

The activity in Phase Two is often mistaken for the change the organization desires. The change management emphasis is thus to keep the organization learning. The activity is not the change; it is moving toward the change. The change will start to occur as people begin to act differently. Just because committees are formed and training takes place does not mean anything has changed. The real changes occur more slowly, when the participants in the process begin to feel free to initiate organizational changes because they improve the system or are just the right things to do. In Phase Two the coordinator will be very busy. It is important that both the coordinator and the organizational steering committee continue to keep a larger perspective.

Phase Three is organizational adaptation. It occurs when the activity focus of Phase Two starts to take a back seat to the problems and difficulties that arise as the organization starts to live with its new choices. As the change process emerges, what was wrong with the organization—the impetus for the change—starts to surface and gets dealt with. What characterizes this phase depends on what the initial diagnostic found and on the specific problems of the organization. Typically, problems and opportunities will arise in each of the areas where emphasis and people are organized to help change the organization (i.e., communication, teams, management, and other special issues).

The change management emphasis in Phase Three is more complex than in any of the previous phases. In this phase the organization has tremendous opportunity; however, the opportunity is veiled in complaints and unrest. Because many of the practices and systems of the traditional organization are no longer acceptable, a great deal of pain is felt throughout the original systems. People complain about shifts in power and resources, about the injustice of the human resource systems, about having to do things differently, and about the whole change process taking too long with few, if any, results. These complaints and others are normal and should be viewed as a good sign. They mean that the organization has opened up and is now ready to start to do things differently.

The problem is that people do not know what to do. Here is where the organizational steering committee, business-unit-level steering committees, and coordinator(s) will earn their money. Not only do they all have to view the complaints as opportunities, they must help and empower people to try new things. This may be the most difficult aspect of the change process yet. People resist the new. Even if the old way is unfair, does not work, and everyone complains, it is hard to get more than just a few people to do anything about it. Nevertheless, the change managers must find a way.

Phase Four is renewal. After the organization has lived with the change process a while and people become somewhat accustomed to making changes, there comes a period when focus is usually lost. It is a time when the original implementation (activity) goals of the change process have been met and when the people staffing the change infrastructure are getting tired. People want off their committees, and everything seems to flounder for a while.

The change management emphasis is critical in this phase. Often the only thing wrong with the process is that the original goals of implementation have been reached and people lack the next clear direction. This, then, becomes the time for renewal. Renewal can be characterized through assessment, alignment, and adjustment. This phase becomes the opportune time for a reassessment based on the original diagnostic instrument. "How far have we come?" is a great question to be asking at this time. Moreover, the time is right to revisit the vision and see what activities now seem appropriate to implement. Finally, it is an appropriate time to revisit all of the change infrastructure. Are the committees/teams focused and doing what will match the new direction? This is an exciting time, when people and the change process often renew their energy.

Phase Five is organizational maturity and performance. This phase occurs when the new organization becomes the status quo. In this phase the change process will be winding down and will either evolve into the next generation of change or will come to an end. Emphasis for change management comes in the graceful and seamless dissolution or evolution of the change infrastructure. By this time the infrastructure should be self-organizing anyway, but, there may still be some aspects or committees that have outlived their usefulness. It is now that these old structures should be nudged into closure.

Joint Summit Meetings

The organizational steering committee periodically calls a meeting of all the individuals involved in

managing the change process. Such meetings are
used to review the change process and to create a
future direction.

At times during the change process it will be appropriate
to bring all the change management parties together to
review the change process history and to create a future
direction. Joint summit meetings include all participants
who are involved on committees or in some decision-
making capacity. These summit meetings offer an opportunity for the key stakeholders of the change process to
come together and discuss the history of the change, the
current state of affairs, and the future direction to take.
Such meetings may have other purposes, but above all
they present a great organizational learning opportunity.

Joint summit meetings can be as short as four hours or
as long as two days, depending on the reason for the
meeting and the purpose or tasks at hand. Summit meetings are officially called by the organizational steering
committee but may be initiated by the coordinator(s) or the
business-unit-level steering committees.

Joint summit meetings are wonderful opportunities
for strategic planning, data collection, issue generation,
change process alignment, and leadership development.
Figure 6-2 is a sample outline for a joint summit meeting.

Role of the Organizational Steering Committee

A key role for the organizational steering committee is
to provide active direction and support in the change
process. Responsibility for ensuring that change management is discussed can be shared by the entire
committee, can be rotated among individuals on the
committee, or can be given to the change coordinator.

Purpose:	Review progress in the change effort.
	Identify major learning.
	Plan (revise) the future of the process.
Membership:	All steering committee members and internal staff.
When:	Six to twelve months into the process and every six to twelve months thereafter.
Duration:	Four hours to two days.
Agenda:	I. Review of the history of the process
	II. Report on major events and outcomes
	A. What occurred
	B. The outcomes: positive and negative
	III. Assessment of strengths and weaknesses of the process
	IV. Lessons learned from the process
	V. Planning for the future
	A. Stop doing...
	B. Start doing...
	C. Do differently...

Figure 6-2. Outline for a Joint Summit Meeting

In general, the role of the organizational steering committee is to set policy for the organizational change process and to oversee the change process. In many respects "oversee" is too vague a term when it comes to change management. The organizational steering committee should not just be a passive group who discuss issues, revisit policies, and hear briefings. A key role for the committee is to direct and support the change process. The committee must keep a finger on the pulse of the process and actively intervene when and where necessary. For example, if the change process seems to be stalling, the committee can ask the business unit steering committees or other interested parties for help. If, on the other hand, the change process is creating too much stress on the current organization or is taking too much time away from the basic business, the steering committee may call for a reduction in the number of meetings or a pause in the training process.

Thinking in terms of change management means that the steering committee members must concern themselves with how the change process is unfolding. In every steering committee meeting the question "How is the change process doing this week (month, quarter)?" should be addressed. Just as a plant or branch manager might ask how the plant or branch is running, the organizational steering committee must track how the change process is going. Figure 6-3 offers some guidelines for this tracking process.

Should there be one person in charge of the change management agenda item? Maybe. But on the other hand, things sometimes get lost when an entire committee is responsible. It is a good idea to identify a change management position on the committee and to rotate that responsibility every six months or so. Another alternative is to

---

1. At what level of maturity is the organization?

2. Are the mission, vision, and values driving new behavior?

3. Is each function of the change strategy working?

4. What problems are surfacing because of the changing activities, and how are they being addressed?

5. If the changes are working, what should we expect to see?

6. If the changes are not working, what should we expect to see?

7. Is there a need for any additional activities or involvement?

8. What barriers have we encountered, and how have we responded to them?

9. What have we learned that we did not previously know, and how has that changed the way we do business?

Figure 6-3. Questions to Consider in Change Management

charge the internal coordinator(s) with the change management role. The coordinator should have mastery over all of the components of the change process anyway. The only liability with this approach is the loss of opportunity for other steering committee members to master all the components of the change process and track the process as a whole.

Monitoring Change

Changing an organization requires knowing not only where it is, but how it got there. A monitoring process can be put in place, but steering committee members must develop their ability to see the change as well.

Ours is an action-oriented society. Most of us grew up in families where the implicit imperative was "Don't just sit there, do something (even if it's wrong)." Not only were we raised on that principle, but most of us are a part of work systems that are based on that idea. Americans have been traditionally rewarded in their careers for behaviors consistent with the action-oriented culture; changing this orientation is not easy.

Traditional organizations are more concerned with where they are than with how they got there. To have any chance of changing an organization and its culture, one must know both. Most high-performance organizations pursuing change processes use some sort of ongoing monitoring process to see whether they are making progress. Unfortunately, they still lack a basic understanding of the culture and of particular problems in a given setting. And as the process goes into place and events begin to occur, steering committee members and other leaders discover that they do not have an "eye" for human systems change like the one they have for their business (task). One way to begin to develop such an eye is through regular assessments of the workplace and the process. Figure 6-4 describes the means for such assessments.

Words of Wisdom

Many lessons have been learned about change and change management. These lessons have been distilled into a few concise thoughts to offer some guidelines in your change process.

The business of managing the change process, like most types of business, is never as easy as it may appear. We

---

Instrumentation

To collect data, use the same instruments (survey forms, interview questions) used in the diagnostic survey. You may have to change some wording to reflect the changes in the population and their preparation. You may want to add scales to give measures of the degree of change in various areas over the period of the process.

Data Collection

Unlike with the original intervention, data can be collected by internal or external people depending on the levels of internal expertise, time commitment, and familiarity.

Data Analysis

To be really effective, the analysis should compare various results from Time I and Time II. Without such a comparison, you lose one of the key anchors needed to assess and understand change.

Reporting

Although the data are for reflective learning in settings such as the steering committee, you should not pass up the opportunity to use this diagnosis as a tool to talk with the work force about what is actually occurring.

Figure 6-4. The Time II Diagnostic for Monitoring Change

have learned some lessons over the years about change and change management that can be distilled into a few "words of wisdom":

1. Everything is connected to everything else. The sooner people in an organization realize this fact, the sooner solution generation (disguised as problem solving in traditional organizations) will be shifted to effective problem-solving and decision-making processes.

2. What goes wrong with the team process is what is wrong in the organization. Trying to implement teams creates problems. It is precisely these problems (the same pathology) that are keeping the organization from moving forward.

3. Problems in the change process are always opportunities for change. Issues raised about unfair and ineffective systems and practices represent a place for improvement.

4. As the heat gets turned up, bubbles occur. As more and more processes are put into place to help the organization change, more and more problems/issues (bubbles) will start to surface. This is good news, as all problems and issues should be seen as opportunities. The question will be whether the organization is willing to understand the bubbles or just wants to destroy the bubble machine.

5. Keep a constant eye on the "stress meter. " One thing we know about large-scale change is that tremendous forces support the organization's status quo. To help the system change, one must also help the system break loose of its ties, a process requiring stress. The art comes in how much stress to apply, where, and for how long. Too much stress

and the system blows apart; too little and nothing changes.

6. Make a conscious effort to develop informal leaders. Although the formal leadership may also need development, a cadre of people just below the surface tend to be your real change agents. It is they who are motivated, see the new vision instinctually, and are listened to by the work force.

7. Don't forget the 80/20 rule: 80 percent of the change process will occur from 20 percent of the population. Concentrate on success. The inverse is also true: 80 percent of your complainers and problems will come from 20 percent of your population. Do not get hung up by the wrong 20 percent.

8. Celebrate small successes. Don't wait for the big ones. Jump on the small successes and make a big deal out of them. This practice sends a powerful message throughout the organization and builds momentum.

9. Use discontent to fuel change. The more pain people feel, the more willing they are to endure change. Lean into the pitch, not away from it, to hit it well.

10. Teach to the top of the class. You have two choices. You can teach to the bottom of the class and bore your top performers, or teach to the top of the class and drag everyone else along with you. We say focus on successful teams, not struggling teams. Focus on small wins, not big problems. Focus on those who can, rather than those who won't. If you teach to the top, everyone learns more.

Figure 6-5 offers an exercise to help you arrive at some of your own "words of wisdom."

In this exercise, write your own "words of wisdom" based on experiences with organizational change. The following questions below provide a way to organize your thoughts.

What lessons have you learned about business and change?

1.

2.

3.

What are your words of wisdom about people?

What are your words of wisdom about change?

What are your words of wisdom about business?

Figure 6-5. Personal Words of Wisdom

7

BARRIERS TO THE CHANGE PROCESS

Barriers to a Successful Process

Barriers to a successful change process are related to external forces, motivation, leadership, and operational factors. Attention must be paid to these barriers to prevent the process from stalling out.

Many barriers can stand in the way of a successful change process. These barriers can come from external forces, or from motivational, leadership, and operational factors. Most organizations will encounter more than one of these barriers during the change process.

If attention is not paid to these barriers, the process will stall. Understanding the potential barriers and addressing them quickly as they arise will keep the process on track.

Barriers are both good news and bad news. They are good news in that they represent the people, processes, and norms that keep the organization where it is. Without these barriers, one would either not have a reason to change or a clear picture of what needs to change. Barriers can be bad news. If they are left unresolved or ignored, they will eventually destroy the efforts to change. Fortunately, the ultimate effect of such barriers is in the hands of the organization's change structure. Figure 7-1 depicts the potential effects of barriers on the change management process.

The following sections describe each of the barriers and provide strategies for uncovering them while minimizing their impact on the process.

External Barriers

External barriers originate outside the organization. These barriers are problematic because the organization has no control over them, yet they will have the greatest impact on the process in the short run.

145

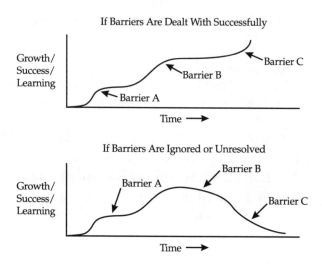

Figure 7-1. Effect of Barriers on the Change Process

External barriers are a result of forces that exist outside the organization. These barriers can be characterized in terms of economic, social, and political factors. Economic factors might include a major downturn in the economy or increased competition in the industry. Social factors might include the move toward diversity in the workplace, the new "work ethic" of young people, and the characteristics of a work force in a given location. Political factors might include government positions on foreign imports, the extent of support for various industries, or the regulatory environment.

Any or all of these factors can directly or indirectly affect a change process. If the economic environment is in a downturn, a company or agency may be less willing or able to support the additional costs of a change effort. Social factors may consume resources and energy or may be a major factor in the motivation of the work force. The political environment influences the other two variables as well as the business directly. A government action may, for example, affect work force morale to the extent that workers are distracted and are uninterested in pursuing major changes in the organization.

External barriers have implications for the change process in two ways. First, the steering committees must be aware of the impact of these variables on the functioning of the business and on the employees. It may be futile to pursue some efforts in the face of major external problems (e.g., trying to make productivity improvements in defense companies while Congress is considering budget slashes). Second, external barriers can explain some of the assessment results obtained. Those assessing progress must be sure to factor in the influence of external forces in determining what went well, what went poorly, and what to do next.

Figure 7-2 provides a work sheet for determining external barriers in your organization.

What are the major barriers (if any) to the change process in the following categories?	What is the potential impact of this barrier?	
	On the organization	On the change process
Economic barriers		
Social barriers		
Political barriers		

Figure 7-2. Exercise for Determining External Barriers

Motivational Barriers

Motivation barriers come from the individuals, groups, and systems within the organization. These barriers can take the form of fear for the loss of power or jobs or can be influenced by reward and punishment systems.

Why is your organization involved in a change process? To increase productivity? to improve quality? to keep the plant from closing? to structure for the future? Whatever the reason, the motivation to change is a product of the current or projected discrepancy between where the organization is and where it wants to be. This discrepancy, or dissonance, drives the change.

Two kinds of motivation can interfere with the change process. One involves people's fears and concerns regarding change; the other is related to existing motivation systems and structures.

Why should people change? Management tends to promote change because "it's the right thing to do. " Others, however, will ask: "For whom?" If, for example, the front-line workers believe that increased productivity or better quality will result in a loss of jobs, they may not share the motivation that drives top management. With a history of feeling "used and abused," many employees will find it difficult to get on board even though they may agree with and support the basic principles behind the strategy.

Middle and first-line supervisors often are less likely to have personal motivation struggles because they believe at some level that "this, too, shall pass." If personal motivation comes into play, it is most often in the form of a fear that successful change will mean a loss of job, because the organization will need fewer layers of management and fewer people to manage those who are there. Or, consciously or unconsciously, middle managers and supervisors may fear the consequences of loss of power. Either kind of fear will cause the instinct for self-preservation to kick in.

Existing motivation systems and structures will more often get in the way of change than reinforce it. For example, we have seen a number of cases in which the management bonus system caused problems. One reason is that most such systems are individually based, not team based, and no thought or effort has been put into being certain that all the individual performance objectives mesh. Thus, for one manager to achieve his or her objectives, something must be done that hurts or deters other managers from achieving their objectives. The other side of the motivation coin for managers is the price (or perceived price) for error. The vast majority of managers and supervisors with whom we work have a long-standing fear of the consequences of error (mostly untested, by the way). As a result, they are generally unwilling to experiment or take risks—behavior that is at the heart of making substantive change. Comparable barriers exist for hourly employees or salaried staff. They, too, often share the fear of error seen in their managers or supervisors.

Incentive systems are often more of a hindrance than a help in change. For example, the steel industry is famous for having paid operators a higher incentive to rerun a coil of steel than they were to run it the first time. In one mill, an even higher incentive was offered for running the coil a third time. In such an environment, getting better quality by doing the job right the first time or by stopping the line and removing a coil known to be bad actually costs workers money.

To get a perspective on the motivators for change in your organization, complete the exercise in Figure 7-3.

A. Motivation for the Organization

    1. What motivates this organization to change?

        a. _____

        b. _____

        c. _____

    2. What motivates this organization to stay the way it is?

        a. _____

        b. _____

        c. _____

B. Motivation for Individuals

    1. What motivates people to change?

        a. _____

        b. _____

        c. _____

    2. What motivates people to stay as they are?

        a. _____

        b. _____

        c. _____

Figure 7-3. Assessing Motivation in the Change Process

Leadership Barriers

Leadership barriers can stop the entire change process. Any leadership resistance must be dealt with
immediately. Failure to do so will give the entire work
force all the evidence they need to conclude that the
change effort is not serious.

Leadership barriers are a result of various people with
power interacting in the change process. Two kinds of
barriers relate to leadership: (1) those arising from what
people do, and (2) those arising from who people are. As
with motivation, leadership can be a powerful asset in or a
major barrier to the success of the process.

Most top managers are goal driven, results oriented,
and highly impatient with long-term change processes.
Their perspectives on the organization's problems are different from the steering committee's, as are their perspectives on what is actually taking place in the organization.
This combined impatience and different perspective make
for difficulties in the change effort. In addition, top managers are typically caught between the expectations of the
powers that be (whether stockholders or corporate leaders)
and of the people in the organization.

Historically, middle managers have controlled information up and down the organization, have used informal systems to get things done when the formal systems
get bogged down, and have used informal reward and
punishment systems with supervisors. This group is
caught between the top managers who control the system
and the people who get the work done. The change process is designed to get at some of the factors that create the
need for middle management's underground network,
informal systems, and so forth. When these old informal
systems are threatened, middle managers will begin to
resist. The power they hold in the day-to-day operation

is tremendous, and rechanneling that power is key to long-term change. In most cases, however, the reconfiguration of the middle is one of the most difficult elements of the change effort. [Note: Some organizations avoid this difficulty by flattening the organization through the elimination of middle management.]

First-line supervisors are another group caught in the middle. The difference between first-line and middle managers is that they have little or no power, and they are where the proverbial buck stops. Unlike the levels above them, first-line supervisors will be affected almost immediately by a team-based process, since they manage the groups involved. The imbalance created by the participation effort creates an immediate reaction, usually in some form of resistance to the change process. As a result, even though supervisors usually have little to protect and are, in many cases, philosophically supportive, they end up being a barrier.

Union leadership is another group with a big stake in maintaining the status quo. Union leaders are both a product and cause of a history of mistrust, hostility, and win-lose interactions. They become a barrier because they, too, are caught between a rock and a hard place. If union leaders suddenly begin cooperating with management (before significant changes occur in the organization), their actions look highly suspicious to their constituents, and the leaders will feel tremendous political pressure (if from none other than their opponents). Yet, if union leaders do not cooperate with the development and delivery of the team-based change process, they will become a barrier. Thus, union leaders are crucial in the change process because (a) they have the power to influence the nature and direction of the effort, and (b) their constituents have the data on what is happening and why.

If the change process is going to be successful, significant changes must occur among the leadership of various constituencies. There are generally thought to be three groups within leadership: (1) those who do not need to change; (2) those who need to change and could change, but may or may not; and (3) those who need to change but will not. The organization already knows who fits into group one. (Interestingly, almost every manager and supervisor believes that he or she is in this category!) The problem at the outset of a process is that it is almost impossible to distinguish between the people who will not change from those who have not changed (but would). Only the process will help uncover which are which. Ultimately, however, a point will be reached where some managers and supervisors cannot or will not make the transition.

Figure 7-4 offers some suggestions for handling leadership barriers.

Middle Managers and First-Line Supervisors as Barriers

Middle managers and first-line supervisors often resent the change process because of power shifts and loss of authority, because of the contradiction between what they are told and the reality they have lived for years, and because two sets of rules exist. For the change process to be successful, their trust and commitment must be gained.

Middle managers and first-line supervisors may pose one of the most formidable barriers to change. For decades, these men and women have been responsible and accountable for achieving the organization's goals. They have labored in circumstances that were almost always difficult and sometimes nearly impossible. And, they have been the

1. Understand and appreciate each constituency's limitations and perspectives.

2. Create opportunities for middle managers, first-line supervisors, and union leaders to expand and redefine their roles and power bases.

3. Create a three-stage plan to help change managers' and supervisors' behavior.

   Stage 1: Define what you want and create ways (e.g., training) to help them get there.

   Stage 2: Generate feedback, coach them, and offer counsel for the right behaviors.

   Stage 3: Replace those who cannot or will not change (they will surface in two to three years).

4. In dealing with union leadership:

   a. Understand the difference between the bureaucratic life of the organizational manager and the political life of a union professional.

   b. Be careful not to get union leaders in a bind between the change process and their membership (while keeping in mind that union leaders, like everyone else, need continuing pressure on them to move in the new direction).

   c. Be patient. Union leaders have little or no reason to believe that this effort is serious. Even if it is, they have no background and little training to prepare them for the effort, and they represent people who do not believe that you are serious or that your intentions are trustworthy.

Figure 7-4. How to Deal with Leadership Barriers

ones blamed and punished for error and failure to achieve objectives, even when the circumstances contributing to that failure were completely out of their control or, worse, attributable directly to their superiors. In one factory, the supervisor described his history in the job as, "I didn't have to think; I didn't have to do anything but what I was told."

Another said, "You just came to work, followed orders, and went home. "

As the change process is implemented, a paradox emerges. On the one hand, middle managers and supervisors are among the first to want things to change. (Although our experience in diagnostic interviews is that they are the groups most hesitant to talk about their concerns, for fear of reprisal. We learn about their true feelings only after some time in the process and they have built up some trust.) On the other hand, middle managers and first-line supervisors have created an environment and management system that gives them control of (often more through informal systems than formal ones) and protection from the organizational environment around them. A change process puts their protective informal structures and systems at risk. They will resist any effort to upset the current balance, regardless of the dysfunction of those systems.

What do they resent about the change process?

- *The power shift and loss of authority.* For decades, first-line supervisors have operated with little or no authority. Most efforts at change and empowerment have been targeted at their work teams, not necessarily at them. They resent being "passed over. "

- *The contradiction between what they are told and the reality they have lived for years.* Supervisors are now being told to "stop the line" if workers report bad quality, to "listen to their people," and to stop being punitive. Their problem is that nobody has even begun to convince them that the same rules apply to the supervisors in relation to their own bosses. Often they are still quietly (or loudly behind closed doors) treated the same way as in the past.

- *Two sets of rules.* Middle managers and supervisors are charged with managing complex problem solving across organizational boundaries still inhabited by other managers and experts who may not share the same values or commitments. Supervisors often know that staff and support areas lag far behind the more visible elements of the workplace in adopting new values and methods.

There are other reasons that middle managers and supervisors pose barriers. The point is that the change process will have to "break the code" of the middle and first-line supervisors and gain their trust and commitment in order to make the shift. To assess barriers at this level in your organization, use the questionnaire in Figure 7-5.

Operational Barriers

Operational barriers arise from pressure to show results, redistribution of power and control, and redistribution of turf and territory.

About the longest period of time change managers will be allotted to deliver some results is twelve to eighteen months. The business has quarterly business reviews, monthly performance goals, and other time-based checkpoints. These checkpoints put tremendous pressure on the organization to produce visible evidence that the change process is working. If and when it does not (and the likelihood is that it will not in the short run), top management will apply pressure to get things moving. Although pressure from the top may provide some motivation to move forward faster, it has a greater potential to get in the way of progress. The need and desire for results in the short term may become one of the most formidable barriers

1. How will middle managers react to the change process?

   a. What will they say about the change effort?

   b. Does what they say differ from what they really feel? How?

2. How will first-line supervisors feel about the change process?

   a. What will they say about the change process?

   b. Does what they say differ from what they really feel? How?

3. What do you think will be the top three biggest barriers for your managers and supervisors when starting the change process in their area?

Managers	Supervisors
a.	a.
b.	b.
c.	c.

4. What can you do to help these managers and supervisors work through their difficulties?

   a.

   b.

   c.

5. If the managers and supervisors decide to go along with the change process in public but resist covertly in private, what signs will you see that will suggest less than full commitment?

   a.

   b.

   c.

6. What strategies can you use if your managers or supervisors covertly resist the process?

Managers	Supervisors
a.	a.
b.	b.
c.	c.

Figure 7-5. Assessing the Barriers for Your Organization's Management

change managers face, because the temptation is to do things to look good. What is worse, there may even be a period in the early stages in which the organization's performance slips below previous levels. Unless this drop is anticipated and leadership is prepared, overreaction to the slippage can cause serious problems.

Redistribution of power and redefinition of boundaries in the organization will generate some chaos. As the instability begins to emerge, key constituents will react with subtle, even perhaps unconscious, strategies to maintain the status quo. Union leaders are usually less subtle than managers. If they want to move back a bit toward the status quo, they will most likely profit the most (politically) by doing so publicly and with some flare. Managers, on the other hand, can be equally forceful in their affirmation of the status quo but will tend to be more subtle in their efforts. The early reactions to power and boundary shifts will represent a major barrier for the organization in its effort to change.

Closely related to the power and boundary issue is the redistribution of organizational turf. This barrier is the result of the redistribution of expert power and information and the sharing of dysfunctional territory. Even though this is one of the most serious barriers, it will be difficult to see until you actually get a number of teams (twelve to fifteen) in place and operating. You will see how teams who want to cross the old, traditional boundaries encounter difficulties.

Here, you also begin to see the principle that what is wrong with the organization will likely become what is wrong with the change process. The "disease" will attack its potential "healer. " When this happens, some will conclude that the strategy is the problem rather than the solution. The challenge will be to separate what is problematic in the strategy from what is problematic in the organization. As this occurs, though, the change process becomes a powerful system diagnostic tool if change managers learn to watch and listen carefully to what is going wrong and what is going right. The extent to which one cannot separate system problems from problems with the process is the extent to which the existing pathology becomes a major barrier.

Figure 7-6 offers a strategy for dealing with operational barriers.

Here are some things to do when the change process starts to run into trouble because of one or more operational barriers. As you do the following, they give the change process "immunity" to the pathology.

1. Look for and talk about operational barriers at every stage of the process, especially up front in events such as orientations, awareness sessions, and management meetings. Later, use arenas such as steering committees, newsletters, department meetings, and summit meetings to discuss them.

2. Call it as it happens—good or bad. When the barriers begin to emerge as problems, use your communication systems to talk about what is occurring. Be careful not to blame or embarrass. Neither is good modeling behavior. Talk about the situation publicly so that people know that you know what they know (and because it raises credibility). Second, by talking about the issue publicly, the employees may begin to believe the organization is serious about doing something.

3. Deal with systemic issues when they are identified. This does not mean that steering committees should go on "witch hunts." Rather, it means they should engage in systemic problem solving as the issues arise.

Figure 7-6. Overcoming Operational Barriers: The Immunization

8

ORGANIZATIONAL LEARNING

The Learning Curve Dilemma

The learning curve refers to the rate at which the
organization transforms as a result of the formal process and related efforts. Change managers should not
except learning to occur in a straight line that reflects
constant, steady growth. The organization more likely
will go through an extended period without any significant indication that change is occurring. Or, for a while
it may progress and then go two steps backward.

Somehow most of us have learned to think of learning and
improvement in terms of an arithmetic line on a chart. We
envision constant, steady growth as a function of time.
However, experience in real organizations has shown that
positive change is anything but steady and continuous.
Hence, the concept of the learning "curve."

Anyone who enters the organizational change process
thinking that improvements will be continuous during the
first two or three years is going to experience a lot of
frustration. Change managers can save themselves some
pain and disappointment by being realistic about the slope
and shape of the curve for learning and change. Figure 8-1
contains three curves representing change in the organization. The first is what change managers hope will happen;
the second is what they expect will happen, and the third
is what is more likely to happen. Without a doubt, an
organization will go through an extended period without
any significant data that regular changes are occurring.
Then, after patience and hard work in the right direction,
a "pop" will occur in the system. That pop is an indication
that learning is occurring.

In the meantime, however, change managers will be
subject to pressure and "noise" about the apparent lack
of progress. Included in the pressure will be recommendations to "stop wasting time and money and get back to

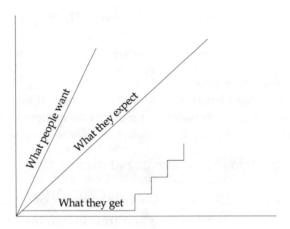

Figure 8-1. Organizational Learning Curve

the business," or to do something different to generate success.

Neither quitting nor changing course is a good option. Most organizations walk away from a change process too soon. That is not surprising, given a long history of broken promises and ineffective efforts. When doubts are expressed about the futility of the effort, there will always be some who take no responsibility for various constituent's contributions to the situation. Often, the walking away is in the form of adopting the latest program to hit the market.

Nothing in the pattern of change fits the expectations for linear improvement in modern organizations. The result is a conflict between how managers think day-to-day and what they need to help them understand organization change.

When the first signs of stall-out appear, the organization change infrastructure should take responsibility for moving the process forward. Here are some options for change managers.

1. They can take the "temperature" of the process—visit teams, do a minisurvey, hold a "summit meeting," or celebrate successes to date.

2. They can determine whether the teams are at a plateau and if so, why. Is there something in the organization blocking their performance? Are they ready to move to the next level of growth and development? In either case, change managers should take corrective action and tell the whole organization what they did.

3. They should just keep on keeping on—take a breath; wait it out. If managers choose this approach, they should listen carefully to the organization and the process to be sure it's the right move.

We should not rule out the possibility that either the organization is not ready or willing to change or that the wrong strategy is being employed. The steering committee should explore such a possibility, but know going in it is the least likely option.

High-Performance Organizations: Two Types of Learning

Organizational learning is the ability of an organization to modify the way it functions based on experience. Two types of learning, adaptive and insight (or generative), are characteristic of long-term change.

Learning is vital to the ultimate change of an organization, yet it is a difficult concept to understand. Robert Shaw and Dennis Perkins (1991) define organizational learning as "the capacity of an organization to gain insight from experience and to modify the way it functions according to such insight. "

Peter Senge (1990) expands the notion of organizational learning by distinguishing between *adaptive* learning and *generative* learning. According to Senge, adaptive learning is "survival learning," characterized by adjustments and changes related to the day-to-day business. It is short-term problem solving. Generative learning, on the other hand, is the heart of an organization's ability to create a different paradigm. The differences between these two types of learning are illustrated in Figure 8-2.

The two types of learning represent very different things for the organization. For example, it is possible for an organization to be good at adaptive learning (making minor adjustments to error, pressures, or opportunities) and remain pretty much as it is. The overall culture, structure, functions, norms, and procedures remain stable. The organization learns only enough to solve a current problem, get rid of a pressure, or capitalize on an opportunity.

Generative learning, on the other hand, implies major, permanent shifts in the organization. This type of learning includes the ability to understand and manage change, not just to solve complex problems. It involves the ability to see the organization in new ways, to discover the problems behind the symptoms, and to invent creative solutions. Many of the change efforts of the eighties reflected only adaptive change, yet the long-term viability of organizations require both adaptive and generative learning.

As organizations progress along the learning curve, evidence of generative learning will take three forms:

- *Change in fundamental beliefs or behaviors.* Some kind of fundamental change occurs in the system (structure, function, beliefs, behavior) in response to forces that are creating an imbalance, jeopardizing its existence. Such changes go beyond day-to-day problem solving.

Adaptive Learning

This kind of learning results from day-to-day adaptation and problem solving in organizations.

Example: A task force was working on the problem of poor morale among salaried workers. One factor contributing to the morale problem was the employee belief that most job openings were "wired"—that is, the management had someone in mind for the job when it became available and was not interested in finding the best person. Their evidence was the fact that (a) salaried job openings were not publicly posted, and (b) the personnel office typically allowed the minimum time from approval of the opening to filling it, so that few had a chance to apply. This practice struck at the heart of equity and justice issues in the minds of salaried employees. After a long, hard fight (mostly with corporate management), the task force was able to get the company to change its approach to salaried openings by posting notifications of openings and conducting more open searches for people to fill them.

Insight Learning

This kind of learning comes from insight about how the organization runs and what really gets in the way of excellence.

Example: A manufacturing organization needed a significant breakthrough to stay in business and remain competitive. They decided to try a team-based process to start a focused-factory operation inside an existing plant. The focused-factory concept required redefinition of work roles, new forms of supervision, different reward systems, and different assumptions about employees. The process, though difficult, was so successful that the factory adopted a team-based approach to the design of all new work areas. As the steering committee and management teams began to compare the positive data from the focused-factory experiments with the negative data from diagnosis of the existing system, they gained insight into the fundamental differences. This process resulted in a major shift in the way the plant managed its business.

Figure 8-2. Examples of Adaptive and Insight Learning

- *Permanence.* The changes in the system are not just temporary adjustments to a certain condition but are permanent changes that result from insight gained from a range of experiences.
- *Success.* Over time, the organization will begin to perform better as a result of the changes.

The key to change is not only to focus on day-to-day problem solving but to watch for patterns of problems and larger systemic issues and go after them.

Adaptive Learning

Adaptive learning occurs through monitoring, feedback, and corrective action. In the transformation process, this type of learning addresses the work or task portion of the business.

Adaptive learning related to day-to-day problem solving requires (1) a feedback mechanism that indicates when something is not going well (e.g., the monthly profit statements, employee attendance figures, customer complaints, grievances), and (2) some kind of change that results in the system behaving differently, thereby reducing the discrepancy between what is desired and what is being obtained. Adaptive learning most commonly occurs through some form of problem solving associated with difficulties or issues. A simple model of the stages of the adaptive process is shown in Figure 8-3.

There are two concerns about the role of adaptive learning in organizational change. The first is that the organization might confuse inventing solutions (only one part of problem solving) with learning. The second is that the organization might not distinguish between adaptive learning and insight (generative) learning.

The managers in many organizations constantly invent solutions to problems. That is, an individual or department goes directly from problem to solution and skips the analytic middle steps. This often leads to the "Ready-Fire-Aim" syndrome, in which a problem reappears over time until someone finally hits the target with the correct solution. This is not the same as adaptive learning; it is merely a form of trial-and-error behavior.

When the organization does not distinguish between adaptive learning and insight learning, it tends to focus on the former to the exclusion of the latter. The result is a constant flurry of fixing problems or responding to pressures with little thought to the real problem, and there is no insight gained from the pattern of problems that occur. If the focus remains on problem solving (adaptive learning), the fundamental paradigm stays in place and little or

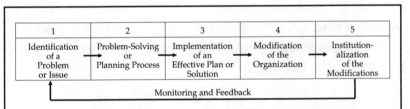

1. Identification of a problem or issue: The problem or issue is named and defined.

2. Problem-solving or planning process: This step includes such things as analyses, alternatives, choice, implementation plan.

3. Implementation of an effective plan or solution: The solution or plan is actually implemented.

4. Modification of the organization: If the plan or solution is effective, the results (learning) are expanded to other areas.

5. Institutionalization of the modifications: The experiment becomes the norm, and what was previously new is just a part of doing business.

Figure 8-3. The Adaptive Learning Process

no significant change occurs. Actually, when an organization begins to understand how dysfunctional its problem solving is and makes changes accordingly, it is experiencing a form of insight learning.

The major shift from almost exclusive focus on adaptive learning in the traditional organization to the more complex (insight) learning that must occur in the change process is a product of (a) creating teams and committees that look at patterns, not just at problems, and (b) creating structures and activities that lead to insight and substantive change.

Most of the learning in organizational change takes place either in the steering committees or in management teams. The challenge in both structures is to stay focused on the issues so that problems get solved without losing sight of the overall process and goals. To meet this challenge, steering committees need to ask not only what caused a particular problem but also why this type of problem keeps appearing and why it does not get solved by the existing organization. They have to learn to see the forest and not just the trees.

Insight Learning

Insight learning occurs when individuals and groups rise above specific issues and begin to look for root causes and variables creating a pattern of conditions. Reflection is key to this process and leads to an understanding of the relationship between action and outcome.

When it comes to insight learning, change managers are not so much interested in the solutions to specific problems as they are in why these types of problems do not get solved or, when they appear to be taken care of, why

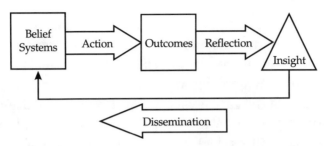

Figure 8-4. Insight Learning and the Organization Behavior Model*

they reappear time after time. Types of issues to address include why what seem to be simple problems do not get solved at the level where the work gets done; why quality does not improve; why the work force does not seem to care about the fact that the business is on the verge of closing due to competition, and so forth. In insight learning processes, the organization is beginning to look at and understand what is occurring, why it is occurring, and what to do about it.

One key to insight learning is reflection. Shaw and Perkins (1991) offer a perspective.

> Effective learning occurs when people effectively reflect on the consequences of their actions and by that gain insight (a richer and more accurate understanding of the key factors in their environment). This is particularly important in understanding cause and effect linkages. The relationship between actions and outcomes is complex and often subjective. Still, effective reflection can add to an individual's existing knowledge base and result in a better understanding of the relationship between action and outcomes. (p. 2)*

*Source: Robert Shaw and Dennis Perkins, "Teaching Organizations to Learn," *Organization Development Journal*, Winter 1991, pp. 1–12. Used by permission of Organizational Development Journal, OD Institute, 781 Beta Drive, Suite K, Cleveland, OH 44143.

Insight learning has potential to occur when individuals and groups begin to understand (1) the interconnectedness of all the stages in the behavior model and the relationship between elements of the model and culture, constituencies, reward systems, and so on; (2) the relationship between a pattern of problems and such factors as out-of-date filters, lack of an adequate range of knowledge or skills, and, most important, the fundamental or core beliefs undergirding the entire organization. The key to insight learning is to structure and support the change process so that it promotes understanding of these two principles in your organization.

Encouraging Insight Learning

Encouraging insight learning in the steering committees involves implementing a new approach to organizing and operating meetings. This can be done through focused agendas, communication, and creation of learning events.

At the outset, most steering committees will try to structure and operate using the traditional management model. They will do planning for an event, argue about issues, and make problem lists. This behavior is predictable because it follows the model with which people are most comfortable. In this case, it is the managers on the committees who typically drive the behavior of the steering committee. (Union members or employee representatives will often define the content with issues.) Because the traditional model alone (consisting mostly of reporting and task-oriented problem solving or "solutioning") is not very effective in insight learning, a different kind of approach is needed for the committees. Here are some ways to help develop a new approach.

Changing the Meetings

As the steering committee moves from the design to the implementation to the monitoring/support stage of the change process, the focus in meetings goes from structuring to implementing to learning. Although some part of meetings will always be devoted to tracking the process (what's going on where), the key to learning is to see the patterns in the tracking. Agendas should focus on what is occurring in the larger sense and on what it means both about the current organization and the organization the committee is trying to create. As the committee begins to see patterns (e.g., there always seems to be relationship problems in certain areas with certain managers), they can begin to problem solve at the system level.

Communication

The steering committee needs to tell the organization about what is occurring and what the change managers are learning about what is occurring. Both good and bad observations should be included. Second, the committee should try to report on both reflective processes and what they are learning from their efforts to change the organization. Committee members should communicate not only facts but also how they *feel* about what is occurring. In this way the organization begins to see the committee model a different kind of behavior and begins to have a new way of looking at itself. (The organization's response to this kind of openness and honesty is often the basis for some insight learning and a paradigm shift.)

Learning Events

The committee can create insight learning events. For example, the committee can hold a "summit meeting" (see

"Joint Summit Meetings" in Chapter 6), consisting of the organizational steering committee and all the business-unit-level or area steering committees. In a summit meeting, the various committees come together for a day to talk about (a) what has occurred over a period of time, (b) what they have learned (insight) from those occurrences, and (c) what they need to do to continue the learning curve. The organization should have such an event at least once a year.

A second kind of learning event is a "learning debriefing" session. It is a structured organizational learning activity conducted after an event in which decisions or other actions have produced very positive or very negative outcomes. Figure 8-5 outlines how to do a learning debriefing session.

Everyone in the organization is responsible for insight learning. One major purpose of steering committees is to experiment with generative learning activities, to gain insight from such activities, to translate that insight into organizational improvement activities and, finally, to transfer that learning to other roles and settings.

I. Why Conduct a Debriefing?

Events that succeed or fail bring out the best and the worst of the organization, and key players tend to create their own (correct or incorrect) views of both what happened and what should have happened. When nothing is done either to reduce discrepant perceptions or to agree on what ought to be done the same or differently in the future, the same cycle is likely to recur (in negative events), and the organization may fail to do something that led to a positive outcome.

II. Who Ought to Be Involved?

The debriefing should include all the key players, from hourly employees to top management, who contributed something significant to the event. Bringing together all the key players at one time will allow the group to compile and compare different views and to decide jointly how to talk about the learning throughout the organization. (Note: This could be as few as four people or as many as twelve.)

III. When Should It Occur?

The debriefing should be held sufficiently long after an event for the proverbial dust to settle but not so long that significant forgetting occurs. One to three months is appropriate.

IV. What Happens in the Debriefing?

First the goals and ground rules are spelled out, then the rest of the agenda follows. Here are some typical ground rules.

1. The purpose is to understand the past and to plan how to perform better in the future, not to blame.

2. If mistakes were made, so be it. We'll own them, understand the basis for them, and try not to repeat them.

3. How the participants will communicate what occurred in the session to the rest of the organization will be part of the task of the day.

V. What Is the Agenda?
   A. Establishing a goal and ground rules.
   B. Mapping the event.
   C. Analyzing good news/bad news.
   D. Deciding what to do differently in the future.
   E. Deciding how to talk about the event to others.

Figure 8-5. Learning Debriefing

CONCLUSION

The contents of this book may seem overwhelming to someone thinking about or engaged in an organizational transformation effort. We prefer an approach that emphasizes the complexity of transformation to one that makes the process appear more simple than it really is. As we move among private and public sector organizations and the unions that represent them, we find a tendency to approach the task of transforming the organization on the basis of a simple cause-and-effect model. This approach usually involves inserting some kind of program into the complex organizational milieu. As one client, with a background in environmental biology, said about this approach: "That's like putting a quart of purifier in a large, polluted pond. There is not enough purifier to make a difference. So, in the end, the pond just pollutes the substance you put in to purify it." That's what we see time and time again. Organizations and leaders who genuinely want to change old models of work and old paradigms of managing attempt to do it by a single or dual strategy (e.g., quality teams, newsletters, business information meetings), each of which may be a necessary condition for change; none of which is sufficient to make the change permanent.

If this book does nothing else, we hope it provides a perspective beyond that employed in the simple cause-and-effect approaches. The topics covered in this book represent all of the things you have to think about when considering what and how to transform an organization. Even then, the book is not a solution in itself. No two organizations are enough alike to make a "cookie cutter" approach viable. We believe leadership has to take a set of principles and strategies, mix them with a high degree of commitment and risk-taking, add some good intuition and orchestration, and season with a little luck to get to where you want to go.

In this work, we took an organizational perspective to the challenge of transformation. This ignores a significant body of literature and considerable emphasis on the role of the individual in the organization. We have not dealt with issues of personality or personal style, of knowledge and skills, or of values and beliefs of the individual. All of these play some role, especially among the leaders of the major stakeholders. We assume, for example, that it is difficult if not impossible to transform an organization headed by someone who does not believe in or who will not actively support the process. At the same time, a single individual has little chance of major transformation without the support, cooperation, and assistance of the people who dwell in the organization day to day.

We do not know nearly all there is to know about how to transform organizations, even if we sometimes act as though we do. There is increasing evidence from a variety of fields from physics to family therapy that a systemic view of organizations is essential and that any attempt to transform organizations must account for the major variables involved as well as the complex interaction of those variables. One camp of critics will ask: "How do you know? What is your evidence?" On one hand, that is exactly the right question. Too often we chase the wind with the latest program. Unfortunately, there is not a lot of evidence—generated in the classical model—to support some of our contentions. At the same time, we believe that the classic model of knowing in the form of the scientific method may not provide a valid or viable vehicle for isolating all that is true. There are just too many variables and too many combinations and interactions of those variables. On the other hand, if an organization is going to wait until there is solid, scientific evidence for what to do, the light at the end of the tunnel will fade into darkness. That is why the experience of external consultants working with transformation and the intuition of consultants and leaders, neither of which is typically measured as part of the classic scientific assessment of change, seem important. Moreover, if change is indeed taking place, it will show up in the organization's traditional performance measures within one to three years.

With all the tools at hand, there is still the challenge of orchestrating the effort. A recipe or a lock-step approach will ignore the nuances and subtle opportunities of the particular organization. Understanding those opportunities and being able to respond in an appropriate and effective manner is key to impacting the organization. This is the challenge for change management leadership. It is also the place where the collaboration of top leaders—management, staff, and labor—will produce a synergy for transformation unlike that available from a single group or individual.

The quality of our future depends on our ability to meet the challenge of transforming our organizations. The experience to date strongly suggests that we can make a difference if the strategy is right and if we are persistent in the face of resistance.

APPENDIX A
PUBLIC VERSUS PRIVATE
SECTOR CHANGE

Some significant differences appear to exist between team-based change processes in the public sector and those in private sector organizations. Although much has been done in and written about the change process in the private sector, much less is known about the process in the public sector. This section touches on some of the major issues involved in addressing change in the public sector.

What Drives Change?

In the public sector, what is the source of the motivation to change? Historically, public sector institutions have been the epitome of a stable-state bureaucracy incorporating only incremental change. We almost never witness large-scale, significant change except in the case of a major disaster, and then the nature and magnitude of the shift is questionable.

Economics and the profit motive are a strong force behind private sector change. Is there something comparable in the public sector? Tom Peters says (in "Excellence in the Public Sector," a video) that the alternative to profit is values. In Peters' view what people believe in and how that translates into work and the quality of life in the organization is the key. If this is true, change efforts have to account for a different system motivator.

In our experience, some segments of the public sector (such as environmental agencies) are heavily values-driven. The tension in such an organization often derives from the fact that the quality of life within the organization is significantly different from the quality of life the organization is trying to create for the public. This dichotomy is the source of a lot of frustration in current total quality efforts. Identifying and addressing such paradoxes can be a powerful motivator for change. Still, this kind of situation is not as motivating as a threatened plant closing or a major layoff.

In public sector processes, high importance is placed on the vision. If the vision is clear and widely accepted, the diagnostic process provides a current baseline against which to compare the vision. The discrepancy between the baseline and the vision (and it will almost always be large) is the dissonance that can drive the early stages of the process.

With the current economic environment, the public sector may be beginning to experience something comparable to what is happening in the private sector. For example, decreasing tax bases (revenues) and taxpayer revolts may create pressures for productivity improvement or more privatization of public organizations. And with the emerging competition in a nonindustrial society, some agencies may find themselves on the verge of extinction. Such movements may create a new array of motivators for public sector change.

Means versus Ends

A second factor that seems to separate the public sector from the private sector is the focus on *means* (what is done or how it is done) versus a focus on *ends* or *outcomes* (what is derived from what is done). The public sector has a history of judging its performance on the basis of means, not ends. The management by objectives (MBO) movement that had its origins in the Department of Defense was a vehicle that reinforced the emphasis on means. Focusing more or less exclusively on means causes the organization to pay attention to what it is doing as the basis for judging success. The number of meetings with citizens' groups, the number of tests done on certain samples, the number of customers served in a certain period, are means-oriented measures.

The alternative is to emphasize outcomes. Education is at the forefront of shifting the emphasis from means to ends. The outcomes-based education movement is driven by a concern with the outcomes of schooling, not just the schooling process. The shift from means to ends will have a significant impact on public organizations, an impact that will surely drive many of these organizations to change efforts.

Emphasis on Social and Political Factors

One of the major influences on the public sector is the government's focus on larger social and political issues. For example, the diversity movement is reflected first and foremost in the public sector, for it is here that politicians and bureaucrats are most quickly called to terms for evidence of their commitment to a social concept.

As a result of being in the public eye, officials feel a strong pressure to respond early and visibly to social and political issues. Thus, large amounts of resources and energy are focused on the particular issue, and objectives are set to provide evidence that the organization is living up to its stewardship requirements.

Many of the efforts related to social and political issues violate some basic principles of change: that everything is connected to everything else and that changing one thing changes everything. As a result, the approach often solidifies existing systems and procedures and merely adds another layer to the existing culture (while calling it "change").

In short, working with change in the public sector is a different process than it is in the private sector. The design, strategy, and management of the process require special sensitivity and actions. Following is a list of suggestions for dealing with change in the public sector.

1. Establish a vision and a values base for change early in the process. Get widespread input to their development.

2. Give special attention to the diagnostic phase, since it will generate the data to establish the discrepancy to drive the process (when you lack economic or performance data as drivers).

3. You may have to adjust the guidelines for the formation of steering committees. There will be very strong pressures, because of a history of misrepresentation and new trends in diversity, for broad representation on steering committees. Although we cautioned against giving in to such pressures in the formation of steering committees, it may be necessary and advisable to consider some alternatives for the public sector.

4. The organizational change communication process is very important. Most public entities focus nearly all their communication efforts on the outside world. If there is much internal communication, the guiding principle is to communicate with

the notion that the outside world will obtain the information. As a result, the communication is often bland, tainted, or irrelevant. In any case, it is always "safe." To drive change—symbolically and in fact—you will need a strong communication component.

5. Steering committees and management teams will need to pay special attention to the issue of motivators. The workers will ask "What's in it for us?" Enthusiasm to become teams may not be widespread, and it may be difficult to construct a situation in which the payoff for pursuing a team-based system is evident.

6. The peaks and valleys will probably not be as great as in a private sector effort, but you may "hit the wall" earlier. Unsticking the process and getting significant movement will present the largest challenge to steering committees.

7. Get political buy off for process and the use of resources as early as possible. You will need the understanding and support later on.

8. Budgeting may be a problem. Often the public sector budget cycle has a twelve to twenty-four-month lag period. The agency most likely did not plan two years ahead for a major change effort, so managers have to scratch together limited resources for the first year and try to hold on until the next budget cycle. Problematic is the fact that early participation and problem solving will require additional resources to implement solutions. Failure to plan for the additional resources could create a barrier to success. (It is one of the factors that reinforces the status quo.)

9. Be aware of internal issues and initiatives already in place that may inhibit or affect the change process—diversity issues, equal employment opportunity/affirmative action, capital expansions, and so on. The organization has only so much energy for human/social systems change, and although all the initiatives are interconnected, it still may turn out to be an emotional or economic zero-sum game.

APPENDIX B
UNIONIZED WORKPLACES

With the decline of the industrial base in the United States, some may think that a discussion of implementation of a team-based process in unionized workplaces is not that critical. Yet it is.

The industrial base in a number of industries has probably declined about as much as it is going to in the next decade. What's left is a strongly organized and very talented work force that is the key to success in the next decade. Beyond that, other segments of the society—notably the service sector and education—are entering an era of organizational change. As this happens, the question of how to involve and relate to unions is a significant issue.

The fundamental issues raised here are

- When do you involve the union?
- How do you involve the union?
- What are you likely to encounter when you create a joint change process?

When Do You Involve the Union?

If you have a unionized workplace and want to effect serious organizational change through a team-based strategy, you must involve the union or unions. To leave them out almost certainly guarantees a failure of the effort and removes the one opportunity the organization may have to alter the future of labor relations.

Some organizations, often those with a tough history with the unions, will involve the union after change managers have thought through the whole question of what to do and have in mind how they want to proceed. This is a mistake. If the labor-management history in an organization is characterized by adversarial relations, mistrust, and varying degrees of hostility, the time to involve the union is at the very beginning. If unions are left out of the initial discussions, two things happen. First, they are more likely than not to assume that this is another company-oriented strategy to weaken or bypass the union. Second, it becomes harder than need be, regardless of their interpretation of management's motives, for the union to join later. This setup invites the response, "If we weren't good enough for you then, we're not good enough for you now."

Moreover, sitting down to discuss the state of the organization, the business climate, and the union's perceptions of the people environment is a unique opportunity to get some of the tough issues on the table. In addition, if as part of the early planning activities change managers attend conferences or visit other locations involved in team-based processes, they should take union leaders along. The common learning experience could go a long way toward eroding mistrust and building a common base from which to launch a process. (Note: Such visits should be to unionized workplaces. Going to nonunion companies is a poor symbolic gesture and puts union leaders in a difficult situation.)

How Do You Involve the Union?

According to some consultants and a lot of managers, the answer to this question is "It depends on how good the relationship is." Wrong. The relationship and past history have nothing and everything to do with how the union is involved. Years ago we talked with a prospective industrial client that was embarking on a team-based process. The managers were looking for a consultant to help with training and wanted our advice on how to proceed. The business was organized by a national industrial union, but managers had provided union leadership with only limited access to the change process. In fact, the organizational steering committee had only one union member, and he was not a top official. When asked why they used this approach, the managers indicated that the union leadership had always been a problem and that they did not want them to "pollute" this process. The one union official invited to participate was the "good guy" among the "den of thieves." These managers were not to be swayed from their view. We declined further invitations to talk with them. This particular company endured a bitter strike a few years later and had little success with its team-based process.

The principle for involving the union leaders is simple: Treat them as full-fledged, legitimate stakeholders in the enterprise and give them an equal voice in the design and delivery of the change effort. The history with the union or management's assessment of the union leadership does not matter. If union-management relations have been adversarial, and if the leadership of the union appears to be considerably different than that envisioned for the process, there is strong reason for getting unions involved up front. If the relationship has been good and change managers do not think having unions involved early on is much of an issue, leaving them out will still give subtle offense. The basic premise is that the nature of labor-management relations will directly affect the change process, so it's a good idea to get the issues on the table and start talking about how to deal with them. Furthermore, managers have no idea of what union leaders are capable of if given a consistently different environment.

What Are You Likely to Encounter?

Here are some of the issues that will arise when unions are involved in a joint change process.

Old Skills in a New Setting

Union leaders bring to the change process all the talent and skills they have developed over the years. Their orientations and abilities, like management's, are embedded in a history of mistrust and anger. They will put these skills into play somewhere early in the process because that's what they know how to do.

What to Do. Relax. The union is also watching managers do the same thing. As trust begins to build and some new skills begin to develop, the behavior of both sides will change (not for everyone, but for the majority).

What Not to Do. Don't make deals early in the process to keep the union in the room. If for some reason union leaders decide to walk out of discussions (usually something has gone wrong in the workplace that is not resolved to their satisfaction), let them go. (Note: We caution unions about using a walkout strategy because that only sets them up for losing face if and when they come back.) Let things cool down and have a discussion about the issue separately from the discussion about the change process. Sometimes as a test of management's good will and sometimes just because it's what union leaders know how to do, there will be a quid pro quo on the table as a condition of participation. The offer should be declined. If management's invitation to participate is not genuine, the union should leave;

if the union wants something (usually in the vein of traditional collective bargaining) as a condition of being there, managers should not give in. It is not a good idea to proceed without the union, regardless of how appealing that may appear. It will eventually be a problem.

The Politics of Unions

Managers seem both unaware of, and ambivalent toward, the political context of union leaders. They tolerate the political machinations of government officials but seem highly intolerant of the same in their union leaders. Perhaps a little time together in a cooperative process will help both sides increase their understanding (and often their appreciation) of the other's context.

Union politics will influence who is named to steering committees, who is nominated to staff processes, what issues get priority, and so forth. This situation cannot be avoided. In fact, the value of the joint process is that the management team can gain tremendous insight into the workings of unions. In return, union leaders develop relationships that facilitate both understanding of the business and day-to-day problem solving in the workplace.

What to Do. Realize that the union's politics are there, are important, and will affect the process in various ways. Learn to appreciate what is going on.

What Not to Do. Don't criticize or get involved in the politics. You'll only create problems. Union politics are a part of the fabric, and managers can only wreak havoc. The leadership of the various factions must be treated as equal partners, even though this will be difficult.

The Threat of the Process on Traditional Union Roles

At some point, usually early in the process, it becomes obvious that the change effort will have as much of an impact on the role of union leaders as it has on managers. At that point some union leaders will resist, just as some managers and supervisors will resist.

The form of resistance varies. One common approach is to try to limit the kinds of issues on which teams can work. Steering committees must always protect the integrity of the collective bargaining agreement and not try to use this process as a way around it. At the same time, if someone wants everything that is mentioned in the contract (such as safety) to be off limits to the team process because it is the union representative's job to take care of such things, you have hit a barrier to change.

What to Do.   Be prepared for the signs of resistance. If you do not get any, you have either a weak union or weak leadership. One of the best ways to handle the impact of the process on the role of union leaders is to deal with it openly and up front in the steering committees. In addition, sessions can be arranged for union leaders to explore their role in the future. Often international union staff representatives are helpful in designing and conducting such sessions.

What Not to Do.   Don't ignore the resistance or try to go around it. You cannot do either for very long. The tougher the resistance, the more it reflects the nature of the day-to-day workplace. This is your big opportunity to try to change it over time.

Labor-management relations have come a long way. In some places, however, labor relations are the same as they were twenty years ago. The team-based organizational transformation process is one of the few environments in which the two parties can sit down together to forge a new relationship and workplace for the future. Managers and union leaders will be amazed at how similar they are in terms of goals, values, and beliefs. In addition, there is rarely any difficulty developing a joint vision both can stand behind. The organization's problems come from the "baggage" of its history, from the two very different definitions of the problem, and from fundamental role distinctions. But this is an opportunity to work on those differences.

SUGGESTED READINGS

Albers, Susan, and Thomas G. Cummings. *Self-Designing Organizations*. Redding, Mass.: Addison-Wesley Publishing Company, 1989.

Block, Peter. *The Empowered Manager*. New York: McMillan Publishing, 1987

Block, Peter. *Stewardship*. San Francisco: Berrett-Koehler, 1993.

Bluestone, Irving, and Barry Bluestone. *Negotiating the Future: A Labor Rerspective on American Business*. New York: Harper-Collins, 1992.

Bolman, Lee G., and Terrence E. Deal. *Reframing Organizations: Artistry, Choice & Leadership*. San Francisco: Jossey-Bass, 1991.

Elledge, Robin L., and Steven L. Phillips. *Team-Building: Beyond the Basics*. San Diego, Calif.: Pfeiffer & Company (in press).

Hackman, J. Richard, ed. *Groups That Work (and Those That Don't)*. San Francisco: Jossey-Bass, 1990.

Harper, Bob. *Succeeding as a Self-Directed Work Team*. New York: HarperCollins, 1990.

Hirschhorn, Larry. *Managing in the New Team Environment*. Redding, Mass.: Addison-Wesley Publishing Company, 1991.

Kanter, Rosabeth M. *When Giants Learn to Dance: Mastering the Challenges of Strategy, Management, and Careers in the 1990s*. New York: Simon & Schuster, 1989.

Kelly, Mark. *The Adventures of a Self-Managing Team.* San Diego, Calif.: Pfeiffer & Company, 1991.

Kinlaw, Dennis C. *Continuous Improvement and Measurement for Total Quality.* San Diego, Calif.: Pfeiffer & Company, 1992.

Kinlaw, Dennis C. *Developing Superior Work Teams.* Lexington, Mass.: Lexington Books, 1991.

Kochan, Thomas A., Harry C. Katz, and Robert B. McKersie. *The Transformation of American Industrial Relations.* New York: Basic Books, 1986.

Kochan, Thomas A., Harry C. Katz, and N.R. Mower. *Worker Participation and American Unions.* Kalamazoo, Mich.: W.E. Upjohn Institute for Employment Research, 1984.

Lawler, Edward E., III. *The Ultimate Advantage: Creating the High-involvemnt Organization* San Francisco: Jossey-Bass, 1992.

Mohrman, Allan M., Susan Albers Mohrman, Gerald E. Ledford, Jr., Thomas G. Cummings, and Edward E. Lawler, III and Associates. *Large-Scale Organizational Change.* San Francisco: Jossey-Bass, 1989.

Nadler, David. *Organizational Architecture.* San Francisco: Jossey-Bass, 1992.

Orsburn, Jack D., Linda Moran, Ed Musselwhite, and John H. Zenger. *Self-Directed Work Teams.* Homewood, Ill.: Business One Irwin, 1990.

Phillips, Steven L., and Robin L. Elledge. *Team-Building Source Book.* San Diego, Calif.: Pfeiffer & Company, 1989.

Reddy, W. Brendan. *Team Building Blueprints for Productivity and Satisfaction.* San Diego, Calif.: Pfeiffer & Company, 1988.

Schein, Edgar H. *Organizational Culture and Leadership: A Dynamic View.* San Francisco: Jossey-Bass, 1991.

Senge, Peter M. *The Fifth Discipline.* New York: Doubleday, 1990.

Shonk, James H. *Team Based Organizations.* Homewood, Ill.: Business One Irwin, 1992.

Tjosvold, Dean W., and Mary M. Tjosvold. *Leading the Team Organization.* Lexington, Mass.: Lexington Books, 1991.

Weisbord, Marvin R. *Productive Workplaces.* San Francisco: Jossey-Bass Publishers, 1987.

Wellings, Richard S., William C. Byham, and Jeanne M. Wilson. *Empowered Teams.* San Francisco: Jossey-Bass, 1991.

REFERENCES

Barker, Joel. *The Business of Paradigms (video)*. Burnsville, Minn: Charthouse Learning Corporation, 1991.

Capra, Fritjof. *Uncommon Wisdom*. New York: Bantam, 1989.

Greeley, Andrew. *Happy Are the Merciful*. New York: Jove, 1992.

Katz, Daniel, and Robert Kahn. *The Social Psychology of Organizations*. New York: Wiley, 1982.

Kuhn, Thomas. *The Structure of Scientific Revolutions*. Chicago: University of Chicago, 1984.

Senge, P.M. *The Fifth Discipline*. New York: Doubleday, 1990.

Shaw, Robert S., and Dennis N. T. Perkins. "Teaching Organizations to Learn," *Organization Development Journal*, 9 (4) (Winter 1991), pp. 1–12.

INDEX